Reaching the Whole Child by Teaching Whole-Class Novels

Indispensable Advice from an ELA Expert

Robert Ward

© Copyright 2019 by Robert Ward

All rights reserved. When forms or sample documents are included, their use is authorized only by educators, local school sites, and/or noncommercial or nonprofit entities that have purchased the book. Except for that usage, no part of this book may be reproduced or utilized in any form or by any means, electronic or mechanical, including photocopying, recording, or by any information storage and retrieval system, without permission in writing from the author.

ISBN: 978-1-6889-8039-6

Cover design by José Lomelí

Contents

Preface: A Love of Literature and the Life Lessons It Provides

Introduction: Reaching the Whole Child................................1

Chapter 1. A Balanced Approach to Teaching Literature......................5
- Pairing Whole-Class Novels with Independent Reading Choice
- Bookmarks and Reading Procedures
- The Importance of Preserving Narrative Fiction

Chapter 2. Recommended Middle-Grades Novels...........................13
- Books about Orphans and Outsiders
- Books about Outcasts and Underdogs
- Expanding the Literary Canon

Chapter 3. Teaching Film as Literature..................................19
- Recommended Historical Films
- Preparing to Teach Films
- Film Versions of Novels

Chapter 4. The Reader's Notebook......................................23
- Table of Contents and Works Cited/MLA Format
- Vocabulary
- Settings and Characters
- Figurative Language
- Citations

Chapter 5. Literary Devices, Predictions, and Taking a Stand...............31
- Literary Symbols: A Reading Treasure Hunt
- Irony
- Foreshadowing
- Predictions: Activating Curiosity and Honoring Student Input
- Taking a Stand: Engaging Students through Controversy
- Placing Everything in Context Organically
- Purposeful, Quality Repetition and The Disadvantages of Piecemeal Planning

Chapter 6. Reading for Analysis and Inference............................47
- The Four Bs of Effective, Expansive Instruction
- Potential Pitfalls of Personalized Learning

- Close Reading and Perceptive Writing
- Comprehending
- Analyzing
- Inferring and Explaining
- Organizing
- Responding

Chapter 7. Whole-Class Literature Discussions……..…………………….....61
- The Difference Between a Teacher and a Facilitator
- Literary Themes
- Class Discussion Prompts for Narrative Texts and Class Discussion Examples
- Paying Attention and Glorious Gold Stars

Chapter 8. Culminating Projects…………………………………………….79
- Ten Book Report Ideas Students Love
- Independent Reading Bookmarks
- The Heroic Challenge and The Super-Ordinary Hero Project

Chapter 9. Collaboration, Inquiry, and Feedback……..……………...………91
- Inquiry Puts Students in Charge of Learning
- Academic Feedback that Works
- The Three As of Meaningful Formative Feedback

Chapter 10. Writing with Passion and Purpose...…………………………….103
- Infusing the Benefit Mindset into the Whole Child
- Communication is Key
- The Good News, Envisioning Utopia, and My Legacy
- Character Therapy and Active Listening Strategies
- Examples of Young Adult Books Suitable for Character Therapy
- Adverse Childhood Experiences (ACE) Test
- Sample Character Therapy Dialogue with Ponyboy Curtis from *The Outsiders*
- Writing from Outside Oneself

Chapter 11. Writing with Sophistication……......……………………………..119
- Writing Complex Sentences Develops Substance and Style in Student Essays
- Writing Responses and Conclusions and The Dreaded Concluding Paragraph
- Twelve Ways to Teach Engaging Titles and Effective Conclusions
- Modeling: Seeing this Activity in Action

Final Words…………………………………………………………………135

References………………………………………………………………....137

About the Author……………………………………………………………140

Preface:
A Love of Literature and the
Life Lessons It Provides

During the initial stage of writing this book, I received the following email from a former student with the subject line that read, "An Old Friend":

Dear Mr. Ward,

I was your English student at George Washington Carver Middle School. I had a great experience in your class! During these past 10 years, I always questioned why it was that your class was the last English class I enjoyed, and it was not until recently that I came across your article "Character Therapy" and I figured out why. Your stories helped me cope with the world as I knew it. Your class took place during a very conflicted time in my life when I did not know my role in society. I did not understand it at the time, but I was really lonely. I had few friends in school but none outside of it. The parks in that part of the city were and are pretty dangerous. It led me to become very introverted. Roll of Thunder, Hear My Cry *and* The Watsons Go to Birmingham—1963 *are two of the many books we read that I felt most connected to, and now I know why. These stories helped me shape and form my identity. You helped me more than I could ever imagine.*

Thank you

While it's always gratifying for a teacher to hear they made a positive impact on a student's life, this young man's words touched me even more deeply than all the other letters and surprise visits I've received from my former students over the last 27 years in the classroom. In this instance, it wasn't just me and my teaching that affected this student's life; it was also the books we read and discussed that brought him solace, wisdom, and hope—especially during those tumultuous years of adolescence and particularly while growing up on the often-fearsome streets of South Los Angeles.

The power of great books to enthrall, uplift, enlighten, and inspire—for literature to literally change lives—is what makes teaching English so gratifying and so important.

After receiving that student's email, I feel more confident and excited than ever to share with you what has worked so well in my ELA classroom with a variety of students—from those with developing to advanced skills, including State-Identified Gifted/Honors students, English Language Learners, and students with Individualized Education Plans, as well as children living in poverty and coping with trauma, both past and present.

I was differentiating instruction before there was a term for it, and I was teaching and reaching the whole child before social-emotional learning ever became SEL.

Staying Gold

In *The Outsiders*, S.E. Hinton beautifully sums up the meaning of gratitude and of appreciating what you have, even if you currently have very little, with two words: *stay gold*.

This is my go-to phrase when I'm issuing friendly caution to a student who's beginning to stray or when I want to celebrate a student who's been especially sensitive, sympathetic, or supportive. My students know exactly what I mean by these two poignant words because together we've explored and discussed a wealth of amazing novels we can compare and contrast, as well as learn from and love.

If I began my teaching career naively (and audaciously) wanting to "save" my students, I now know my true role is to support them in acquiring the knowledge and skills to save themselves—socially, emotionally, soulfully, and academically.

I discovered long ago that merely preaching to my students yields limited results. It's far more fruitful and fun to allow my students to discover for themselves the wisdom to be gained from great stories. Universal themes of thankfulness, perseverance, and self-assurance sustain us through our own hard times and spur us to strive for the things that really matter in life, so much of which is meaningful rather than material.

A consistent, cohesive focus on providing all kids with leadership, love, laughter, and learning ensures that no child feels abandoned or ill equipped to navigate the complexities and challenges that life presents to them. Teaching whole-class novels is a wonderful and wonder-filled way to organically meet the needs of the whole child.

Introduction:
Reaching the Whole Child

Here's my definition of teaching and reaching the whole child:

As I explain in my book *Talented Teachers, Empowered Parents, Successful Students* (Ward, 2017), student academic achievement is inextricably interconnected with a child's growth in social, emotional, and soulful learning. Since each of these core components is no more or less vital than the other three, all four aspects of child development should be addressed holistically and equally, right from the beginning of nurturing and educating each child.

According to the National Commission on Social, Emotional, and Academic Development (2017), "Decades of research in human development, cognitive and behavioral neuroscience, and educational practice and policy have illuminated that major domains of human development—social, emotional, cognitive, linguistic, academic—are deeply intertwined in the brain and in behavior. All are central to learning."

The through line of all my many articles and books has been about balancing these four crucial components in the lives of every child. Honoring and attending to the needs of the whole child has been my mission and remains the only reason why I am a successful teacher today.

The Four Fs of Teaching

For teachers, an effective equilibrium for meeting student needs is found through what I call the Four Fs of Teaching, and these are explained in depth in my first book for educators, *The Firm, Fair, Fascinating Facilitator* (Ward, 2015).

- **Firmness** provides the security, structure, and stability that engender courteous student cooperation and orderly classroom management. Teachers are role models of professionalism and cultivate mindfulness and self-regulation in their students.

  I regularly use the examples found in novels to highlight the benefits of being respectful, responsible, and reliable. This continual reinforcement of interpersonal skills and self-awareness directly contributes to my students' growth in social development.

- **Fairness** fosters the caring, trust, and recognition that support a strong teacher-student rapport. Teachers nurture their students on an individual basis and are attuned, attentive, and accessible so each student progresses toward their full potential and so no child falls through the cracks.

  Books are rife with lessons in self-confidence and compassion. I frequently see students, who initially came to me insecure and guarded, begin to open up and to open their hearts to the needs of others—often matching our literary characters' journeys in discovering their inner strength and unleashing their inner hero.

- **Fascination** delivers passion, purpose, and peer interaction that evoke sustained student investment. Teachers keep their students personally engaged and excited about school and know their students as thoroughly as possible in order to tap into their natural talents and budding interests.

  The unraveling of a long and compelling tale could be the only reason some students return to school each day. I cannot teach and I cannot reach students if they're not here and if they aren't engaged. Masterful stories spark the curiosity and awaken the creativity so vital for development in student self-expression.

- **Facilitation** furnishes inclusive, accessible lessons; rich curricula; and actionable formative feedback that foster increased student achievement and independence. Teachers balance academic standards with scaffolds, strategies, and supports that ensure equal opportunity for all students.

  I've found it's possible to teach every conceivable ELA standard within the framework of whole-class novels and supplementary informational texts. Placing all instruction and assignments within the reading and studying of several novels provides students with a context and cohesion that increases each student's self-efficacy, no matter where their knowledge and skills began.

A firm, fair, fascinating facilitator simultaneously supplies all four of the above groups of indispensable student necessities because every child requires leadership and limits, understanding and encouragement, meaning and inspiration, as well as excellent instruction, in order to thrive. Not only does such a balanced whole-child approach better prepare all students for the rigors of education, it also provides them with a strong foundation for a fruitful and fulfilling life.

Successful teaching isn't *just* about classroom management. As much as some assume, it's not *all* about relationships either. Likewise, it's not *entirely* about engagement. And even though the powers that be try to convince us so, it's not *solely* about standards-based instruction. Such one-sided approaches misrepresent the depth of what every child requires, as well as the richness that resides within each of them.

Great teaching is of course equally about each of these four aspects. We educators are now steadying our course and in so doing earning our students' faith and fidelity. The enduring combination of firmness, fairness, fascination, and facilitation offers every teacher the foundation and flexibility to achieve the greatness that will be recognized and welcomed by students and parents alike.

Similarly, you'll see that I don't *only* rely on whole-class novels to teach and reach my students. Independent reading choice is also a major component of my ELA approach. This book offers teachers plenty of teaching options so they in turn can provide a wealth of reading opportunities for their students.

"Soft" Skills are Actually Substantial and Significant

When it comes to successful and satisfied human beings, be they adult or child, there are no "soft" skills that brought them to and sustain them through such contentment and conquest. The touchy-feely, warm and cozy, fired up and rarin' to go aspects of teaching not only matter, they're essential for deep, lasting learning.

Emotional intelligence, social smarts, and soulful sustenance aren't just fluff to occasionally add to the rigors of education; they're the determining factors between truly fulfilling one's potential and merely marking time until the last bell rings. All four avenues to achievement and self-actualization are connected, complementary, and equally crucial. Therefore, we must no longer diminish the importance of any vital skill by referring to it as "soft."

Moreover, being concerned about and attending to the needs of kids in crisis and those children experiencing undue (and often unimaginable) personal hardships have nothing to do with being soft. If fact, cultivating resilience, hope, and perseverance in all children provides them with the tools that will make them strong enough to overcome any adversity, eventually all on their own. We want to raise children to be strong, not merely safe. The lessons learned through great books is one powerful way to do just that.

Thorough Motivation is Key

Teachers can all at once (and on an ongoing basis) capture their students' hearts, hopes, minds, and manners! Not only is it ultimately possible for every adult in every circumstance to rouse all of this essential motivation in children, it's requisite. For without such a comprehensive approach to meeting children's elemental needs, we cheat kids out of optimal learning experiences and fail to fully inspire the immense promise that resides in each child.

When teachers transform their students' thoughts into actions, they move them from being passive consumers of information to becoming active participants and creative producers of insight and intellect. There simply is no room or rationale for students to be distracted or disruptive when they've been given the essential structure, support, stimulation, and skills to excel.

Experienced educators well know that nothing is a magic bullet—not for closing the achievement gap, not for motivating each child, not for increasing student literacy and instilling a love of reading, not for making every teacher highly effective, and certainly not for curing every social ill. These challenges are too complex to blithely assume we can conquer them all with panaceas, platitudes, or pixie dust.

Nevertheless, doesn't the potent four-part combination of children choosing to act out of mutual regard *and* eager responsiveness *and* deep involvement *and* growing proficiency sound like a much surer and sanity-preserving game plan than constantly battling the all-too-common defiant, distant, disinterested, "don't get it" attitudes many teachers encounter from their woefully unmotivated students?

If you want to create a classroom filled with willingness, wisdom, wonder, warmth, and worth, my whole-child, whole-class novel approach offers you a sound path to do so—all while retaining the freedom to be the unique teacher only you can be, as you inspire and support your students to be the special individuals they all must be.

Chapter 1.
A Balanced Approach to Teaching Literature

English teachers are typically literature lovers, so it's natural for them to share their passion for reading with their students by introducing them to great books. However, some teachers find the prospect of reading and analyzing an entire novel with their classes overwhelming or problematic.

Teachers' most common concerns center around these questions:

- How can I provide choice and accommodate individual interests when my students are limited to reading just a couple of compulsory books?

- How can I differentiate instruction for my advanced and developing readers when every student reads the same book at the same time or pace?

- How can I expose my students to a wide variety of genres, authors, and writing styles when only a few novels are covered in a single school year, just the reading of which often takes up large amounts of precious instructional time?

As I wrote in my *Edutopia* article (2017a) "Getting Everyone on the Same Page," teaching literature never must be reduced to either-or propositions. Instead, provide students with breadth *and* depth, options *and* new opportunities, as well as individualized instruction *and* equal access. Facilitated properly, whole-class novels aren't constricting; they're portals to inspiration, expansion, and empowerment!

For nearly three decades, I've successfully taught whole-class novels right along with assisting my students in choosing their own books that are tailored to their personal interests and abilities. There's room and reason for both approaches, and practicing the reading process together only creates better independent readers and thinkers (Gordon, 2017).

This all begins with knowing what moves your students, while also knowing what moves you as an educator. For when these two potent motivators intersect, teaching magic occurs. Ask colleagues who have expertise with students similar to yours which books their students love. Then read some of those yourself, and teach the ones that speak to you. Use the rest of those recommendations and lists of favorite books (see Chapter 2) as a foundation for your multicultural, multi-genre classroom library and as targeted suggestions for your students' independent reading choices.

With experience, you'll become an artful book matchmaker, skillfully pairing each student's proclivities and proficiencies with the perfect book! And the literary love connections you arrange will bond your students to your class just as much as to their newest beloved book.

A Compelling, Communal Experience

A sense of community and scholarly inclusion is created when students laugh, gasp, and weep in unison while reading the same engrossing grade-level novel (Mizerny, 2106). This literary experience becomes one of not just reading the book together but of collectively *living* the book as the characters, plot, and life lessons unfold and draw students in ever more deeply.

Therefore, I prefer entire books to be read in class, with every student silently reading along with an excellent audio recording of the novel. Only after gaining a clear grasp of what they've read do I assist students in developing their reading fluency by having each student choose a favorite passage to practice and then read aloud to the class.

Do not try to teach reading fluency and reading comprehension at the same time. These are equally important literacy skills, but they must be taught separately. Teaching reading fluency *after* students understand (and love) a chosen passage and have had ample time to practice their passage alone and in front of small groups ensure that student confidence and success will be maximized.

Having all students read along with audio recordings also addresses two common complaints about whole-class novels: Many students won't actually read assigned chapters for homework, and cold-reading the text in class, even when students volunteer, is often a slow and cringe-worthy endeavor. However, listening to articulate, expressive reading performed by a professional actor on a recording is time well spent: It's time thoroughly enjoyed by all (Short, 2019), it literally puts every student on the same page, and it models what reading fluency actually looks like.

And isn't igniting a love of reading the gateway to lifelong learning?

Differentiated Instruction Provides Equal Access

Teachers build community not just through shared experience but also through shared understanding. Whole-class novels provide access to all because no student must completely comprehend everything right from the beginning. If some students struggle with initial confusions about historical context, vocabulary, or anything ultimately crucial to a full grasp of an especially challenging book, they soon find that what may have been confusing at first will become increasingly clear and accessible after frequent, interesting discussions and progressive readings that feature the same settings, characters, plotline, references, and themes.

Along with the arsenal of supports, scaffolds, systems, and strategies described in this book, evolving readers will gradually be able to interact with the text on an equal footing with their peers. And when they do, the boost in their self-confidence is writ large upon their faces. This collective lesson in grit and growth mindset will then be carried over to when your developing readers actually stick with their independent book choices and reap the rewards of reading entire novels all on their own.

Also, an expanding set of common reference points and literary terms with which to compare and contrast multiple novels over time exposes the underlying universality of literature, no matter how seemingly disconnected a new book, whether independent or whole-class, may be at first glance. This overriding sense of cohesion and context imbues your entire curriculum with meaning.

With a great book in hand, it's easy to engage even the most hesitant student, but it's quite another thing to sustain that interest when subsequent assignments and discussions are deeply demanding and increasingly nuanced. Yet when teachers also focus upon every student's need for self-expression by awakening their sense of passion and purpose, students become thoroughly involved and invested. The teaching of whole-class novels fulfills this yearning for significance when teachers choose books that resonate with their students on many levels. The expansiveness of novels, as opposed to short stories, invites a multitude of interpretations and a wealth of personal connections. When teachers provide their students with these meaning-making opportunities, the buy in is palpable and the soulful needs of the whole child are met.

Critical thinking and reasoned evaluation require increasing sophistication, but even developing readers are eminently capable of startling insight and informed opinion—if the teacher has given them the opportunities and encouragement to actually share their ideas. Give kids a great novel, and on a very profound level they all can quite soon bring something to the table, even as the nuts and bolts of reading may still need a little tightening for some.

Pairing Whole-Class Novels with Independent Reading Choice

My middle school students are always in the process of reading *four different books at the same* time throughout the school year. Here's how I accomplish this reading cornucopia:

1.) Major Whole-Class Novels (1 per semester)

I select one major class novel per semester that we read in its entirety and together as a class. I lead the class discussions of these novels, and my students respond to my carefully crafted questions with their insights, ideas, and opinions backed by textual evidence and explanation. As you will see, taking adequate time (sometimes 10 weeks or more) to read and explore these major whole-class novels never becomes tedious because this is only one of four books (two of which are whole-class and two of which are independently chosen) my students are always actively in the process of reading.

Various short stories, poems, songs, non-fiction texts, artwork, and films related by historical period and/or theme supplement these anchor novels. Thus, my students gain experience with many genres, writing styles, and forms of artistic expression. Students also use all of these sources when responding to a variety of essay prompts.

In my classroom, the notion of "forcing" students to read what the teacher somehow demands from on high is transformed into a process of allowing the great stories themselves to entice, inspire, and enrich my students, just as they have for generations. There's good reason why some books become classics, but if a certain book isn't your cup of tea or doesn't meet your students' needs, just choose a different classic or try a contemporary novel surely destined to become part of the young adult canon.

Readings of my whole-class novels range from 15 to 30 minutes. These reading time frames are determined by logical points in the plot for the class to pause and ponder, as well as how much discussion time will be needed to thoroughly appreciate what transpired in the day's reading. These class discussions are structured by vocabulary, settings, characters, figurative language, predictions, and literary devices, all of which are thoroughly explained in the next chapters. Class discussions of each reading section typically last one or two 50-minute class periods.

2.) Minor Whole-Class Novels (4 or more per school year)

In tandem with the two major whole-class novels, I select another in-class novel that has several sequels and that we also read together throughout the year. I usually choose either the heartwarming *Shiloh* quartet of books by Phyllis Reynolds Naylor or the riveting *Hatchet* series by Gary Paulsen. Also, right before winter break we read the hysterically funny and moving book by Louis Sachar, *There's a Boy in the Girls' Bathroom*.

For these minor novels, the students themselves lead the class discussions and use the inquiry process of creating compelling questions to pose to their classmates (see Chapter 9). My mixture of comprehension, analysis, inference, and response questions that guide our class discussions of the major whole-class novels we read serve as an ongoing model for how my students can compose their own probing questions that move the literary conversation forward or below the surface.

Through the student collaborative process and with my feedback and support, each student refines their ability to interact with rich text on a very perceptive and personal level. With these supplemental whole-class books, my role as facilitator becomes one of pointing my students in a (slightly) different direction, filling in gaps, and nudging them towards interpretations they may have missed.

3.) Self-Selected, Independent Homework Books (1 per month, 7 or more per school year)

My students are also required to read at least one self-selected book (pre-approved by the teacher) per month for homework and to complete a book report (see Chapter 8) that mirrors the activities used with our various whole-class novels (Sacks, 2019).

Students must procure these homework books on their own (from the school or public library, from home, or purchased) because I want them to familiarize themselves with the resources available in order to find a book that captivates them and that also matches their current independent reading level. Through the course of the school year, these independent reading books allow me to progressively build each student's reading skills and reading enthusiasm, as well as to progressively challenge them to read longer and more complex books.

This independent reading is my students' only homework for my English class. This homework is flexible in that students don't necessarily have to read every single night; they only need to budget their time in order to complete the book they chose and its related assignments by the end of each month. (I abandoned reading logs, daily reading summaries, and the accompanying parent signatures years ago.) There's nothing more powerful or pleasurable for kids to do at home than to interact with a book they love.

I will not approve books that were made into a movie, however. There are plenty of other amazing books in the genre of their choice without a student being dependent on reading the current box office sensation or a readily downloadable film. This stipulation makes my book report very hard to fake, and I can easily discern when any student hasn't actually read a book. I also do not approve graphic novels or heavily illustrated books. Students are welcome to read these books for their personal pleasure, but these will not be accepted for English homework credit.

Unlike many teachers, I do not "just" want my students to read or to "just" read anything. I want my seventh and eighth graders to approach text (pages and pages of rich, relevant text) with anticipation instead of anguish and with aplomb instead of anxiety. This reading delight is accomplished because time after time I have proven to my students with the novels we read together in class (and they have proven to themselves with the books they have chosen to read at home) that reading is not only worthwhile, it is essential and deeply fulfilling.

4.) Self-Selected, Independent In-Class Reading Books (ongoing)

An additional independent novel is kept *in class* for each student. For this in-class book, my students choose a book from my extensive classroom library, which is organized by genres. I've become an expert at suggesting great books for those students who ask for my advice, and students themselves enthusiastically recommend their favorite novels and authors to their classmates. Students may bring in their own books, but these particular books must be kept in class each day until finished.

These in-class novels are passed out to sit on each student's desk every day. These books are read only during English class (and each day for students in my Homeroom) at various silent reading junctures during the week. They are also to be read as an automatic sponge activity when students finish their assignments early.

Since I cannot control which students actually do their reading homework, having these in-class independent books assures me that every student is indeed reading on their own, several days per week, at their current level, and in a genre they enjoy. I use designated silent reading times to check in with students regarding their comprehension of and satisfaction with their current book, as well as to offer targeted suggestions for their next favorite book. My book recommendations always include the goal of expanding each student's horizons and prodding them to read more challenging and sophisticated novels.

Whenever students finish these in-class independent books and complete the same activities required for home reading, they turn in their book reports for homework credit or extra credit. Because the amount of in-class silent reading time varies from week to week and these books remain in class, students cannot be sure of when they will complete these in-class books and therefore should not depend on them for the current month's homework credit. Nevertheless, the time spent in class reading independently will eventually contribute to a student's grade, and this provides added incentive for them to read diligently during the class time provided.

If they do their homework, each student reads a total of 15 books by the end of the school year, with many voraciously reading 20 or more—over half of which are of their own choosing. In the four ways outlined, I'm able to balance the benefits of cohesion and direct instruction with differentiation and student voice and choice.

A Word about Literature Circles

I've never been a fan of literature circles, so I've never used them. Nevertheless, I have many colleagues who swear by them. If this reading approach is of interest to you, there are many articles and books extolling the benefits of literature circles. However, I believe it's crucial for the *entire class* to have a wealth of common reference points. My major and minor whole-class novels accomplish this with great results, while providing equal access to challenging, grade-level texts for my developing readers.

Bookmarks and Reading Procedures

There's always a bookmark in all of my class texts. This can be as simple as an index card, and it's always handy for students to be able to hold their place in a book as we constantly move from text to note taking during class discussions. I use the following bookmark procedure whenever the class is reading the same text in unison with an audio recording or with the teacher reading large passages aloud. "We are *all* reading. You are never just listening," I remind my students during whole-class readings.

All of my students are *required* to move along their bookmark just under the line we are all currently reading. A few students may initially balk at this structured reading process, but I maintain it's necessary because it guarantees full reading focus. It's also a simple kinesthetic activity that keeps students' hands physically active rather than passive while reading. There's no way a student can fake actually reading while using this effective bookmark procedure. While I'm walking around the classroom, I can determine with just a glance which students are indeed actively reading by virtue of their bookmark being in the same place as everyone else's.

Each time before (and after) we read as a class, I have every student "get up and stretch" in order to refresh and refocus. After they sit back down, I ask my students to "sit up straight as active, attentive readers." I don't want to see students' heads resting on their hands or on their desks while following along with their bookmarks. By properly using these bookmarks, books will be held open with just the right amount of pressure without splitting the spine of our precious books. I certainly don't want to see students' elbows or arms pushing down upon our delicate novels.

A student who disregards my reading procedures one too many times will be directed to read while remaining standing in a designated space at the back of the classroom. I make sure that where I tell the student to stand doesn't allow them to lean on a wall or table. This usually happens only once, as everyone quickly gets the picture that I'm serious about my reading procedures.

The Importance of Preserving Narrative Fiction

Even though there's a movement to progressively limit the amount of narrative fiction as compared to non-fiction that students read, I will have none of it. I advocate for a balanced approach to all aspects of teaching, and this area is no different. Students only study narrative fiction in English class, but they read non-fiction texts in history and science classes all the time. In order to preserve an *overall* reading balance, narrative fiction should actually constitute the bulk of ELA reading.

English language arts class is the only core subject that has *art* included in its title. While there's a certain artistry to non-fiction writing (and I've written five other non-fiction books and over 100 articles), there's no comparison to the imagination, style, and intricacy of writing narrative fiction. If we say we want to cultivate lifelong readers, let's acknowledge that the majority of adult reading will be in narrative fiction.

In Praise of Student *and* Teacher Choice

Just as I honor student reading choice, I also strongly believe individual teachers should have autonomy in choosing which novels their students read as a class. Due to limited resources and to ensure articulation without undue repetition, I understand that English or grade-level departments may need to agree on a menu of novels from which each teacher can choose; but that's about as restrictive as it needs to be. Requiring every student in a school to read a certain novel at a certain time is unnecessarily prescriptive to teachers who know their students' needs, as well as their own needs and proclivities, better than anyone else. Although it's not always easy for a teacher to procure and preserve an entire class set of the same novel, they not only should try, teachers should be fully supported in doing so.

Chapter 2:

Recommended Middle-Grades Novels

My following book list was featured in the U.S. Department of Education's "The Teacher's Edition" newsletter (2016) and is a brief sampling of literary characters who face extraordinary obstacles virtually all on their own.

Books about Orphans & Outsiders

Have you ever noticed that the main characters in a great deal of young adult literature are orphans? It has to be more than a coincidence that the inspiring protagonists of some of the most beloved books from the young adult canon are either parentless or are suddenly isolated from the love and support of family and friends.

1. Ponyboy from *The Outsiders* by S.E. Hinton

Ponyboy ultimately turns the tragedy of the recent death of his parents and three of his peers into a will to help others become less judgmental and to appreciate what they have by "staying gold." Ponyboy also learns how to remain sensitive and sympathetic in a bitter, divided world, as he finally realizes that courage is remaining calm and peaceful while you find solutions that don't involve hatred, violence, or revenge.

2. Harry from the *Harry Potter* series by J.K. Rowling

Harry is orphaned and temporarily trapped in a horrible home where he's unwanted and unappreciated. Harry finds new friends and battles new foes while attending wizard school at Hogwarts.

3. Lonnie from *Locomotion* and *Peace, Locomotion* by Jacqueline Woodson

Orphaned at seven and separated from his sister, who is in a different foster home, Lonnie uses the power of poetry and letter writing to deal with loss and to artfully express his yearning for belonging. These books are perfect for teaching how creativity and the written word heal ourselves, as well as inspire others to persevere.

4. Mia from *If I Stay* by Gayle Forman

The sole survivor of a family car crash, Mia ponders the meaning of life without her parents and brother. Previously an outsider, Mia has an experience that renders her literally outside of her body, providing a perspective that's as agonizing as it is eye opening. Through this metaphysical metaphor, readers join Mia on a journey of heartache that ends in hope.

5. Matteo from *The House of the Scorpion* novels by Nancy Farmer

While trapped in the savage country of Opium, Matt determines he's actually the clone of the evil drug lord, El Patrón. Matt claims his own identity by recognizing that choices, confidence, and adapting to change create true character. Later befriended by a band of fellow orphans, these "Lost Boys" learn that all is never lost as they elude their captors in a thrilling escapade, leaving readers cheering for these resourceful ragamuffins.

6. Jeffrey from *Maniac Magee* by Jerry Spinelli

Orphaned (twice) and perpetually running (from himself), Maniac takes a circuitous route in learning to finally face his fears instead of fleeing or giving up. While showing others that friends and family come in all colors and versions, Jeffrey shatters stereotypes and surmounts segregation. Students will understand that the "knots" of life are untied when we face our painful past and accept the love of faithful friends.

7. James from *James and the Giant Peach* by Roald Dahl

James is an orphan living with his two vile aunts, until he embarks on an incredible adventure with his new insect friends.

8. The Baudelaire siblings from the *Series of Unfortunate Events* books by Lemony Snicket

Three oppressed orphans endure alliterative adventures against the evil Olaf.

9. Dorothy from *The Wonderful Wizard of Oz* series by L. Frank Baum

An orphan girl swept far from home forms friendships, faces witches, and exposes a fraud.

***

Despite their tumultuous journeys, these characters all manage to persevere and to eventually triumph, armed finally with the insight that what they needed most was within themselves all along. This profound and lasting sense of gratitude provides these young heroes with the strength they need to not only survive but to thrive. It is this inner fortitude and grace that assures the reader these characters will be just fine long after The End.

Of course, the crucial lesson the authors of these magnificent books want to convey is universal and elemental: If these *children*, who ostensibly have no one and nothing, can summon the self-control, courage, and determination to slay dragons—fearsome beasts real and imagined, internal and external—then so can you and I, especially those of us fortunate enough to be in far more comfortable and comforting situations.

The list of recommended whole-class and independent student reading books above, as well as the additional list below, serve not only as possible suggestions for your own classroom but as examples of how these seemingly juvenile books address serious issues and offer inspirational ways forward for children and adults alike. Forget about purchasing costly social-emotional intervention programs that try to teach coping schools and a growth mindset (Dweck, 2006). Books like these are all we've ever needed to address the needs of the whole child.

Books about Outcasts and Underdogs

Superheroes and superstars already captivate kids, and many students could teach a master class on these subjects. The fresh perspective teachers can offer is how students *themselves* can and should be heroes. As advocates of the growth mindset, teach children that heroism doesn't require an obsession with perfection or product. When educators also value process and progress, students are better prepared to accomplish honorable acts of their own.

Also, emphasize that heroes include ordinary people who gallantly perform admirable deeds—frequently in the midst of difficult situations or personal challenges. Despite any shortcomings, stumbles, or setbacks, heroes ultimately rise to the occasion and selflessly help others, often simultaneously saving themselves.

Moreover, the hero usually is the only person who could create such a positive outcome in the given situation. If it were not for this unique human being's cunning, courage, and compassion, the world would be less well off. Lessons like these not only teach kids how much potential for growth and greatness actually resides in them, they also show children the benefits of generosity and giving back.

Literary Role Models

Heroic stories teach students about mitigating mistakes, learning from loss, and overcoming adversity, all of which are key elements of a growth mindset (Dweck, 2016). Despite hurdles, heartache, and hardship, literary heroes ultimately leave themselves and humankind in a better place than when they began.

The following list from my article for *Edutopia* (2017b) features diverse protagonists, many of whom reappear in compelling sequels that reinforce lessons learned and keep students hungry for more. While these young adult books are typically middle school level, their resonant subject matter, complex characters, profound themes, vivid vocabulary, and historical contexts make these novels suitable as enriched reading for elementary students and as a bridge for high school freshmen.

Don't let the youth of these protagonists fool you: All of these books, penned by diverse, award-winning authors, are worthy of serious scholarship as they satisfy, stir, and speak to readers of all ages—and upon multiple readings.

1. Kenny from *The Watsons Go to Birmingham—1963* by Christopher Paul Curtis

School bullies and his big brother, Byron, torment Cockeye Kenny; but when a family vacation to the segregated South turns tragic and traumatic, it's By who twice rescues his "baby bruh." Byron gently coaxes Kenny to reconcile with the monsters and angels that nearly destroy him. As Kenny makes peace with life's joys and cruelties, readers realize giving up is not an option.

2. Karana from *Island of the Blue Dolphins* by Scott O'Dell

Orphaned while witnessing the massacre of her father and many of her native island tribe, a young girl is inadvertently abandoned for eighteen years. Yet Karana endures and even thrives by embracing enemies, both animal and human. This profound, beautiful story about the power of forgiveness and the triumph of the human spirit spurs students to summon their inner strength in the face of despair and desolation.

3. Brian from the *Hatchet* series by Gary Paulsen

Brian enlists grit, guts, and the grandeur of nature to come to grips with himself, his parents' divorce, and the harsh wilderness. Equal parts adventure and introspection, these stories instill inner and outer harmony, emboldening students to appreciate what they have and proving just how resilient humans can be.

4. Katie from *Kira-Kira* by Cynthia Kadohata

When a move to 1950s Georgia separates her family from their Japanese community, Katie survives the stigma of bigotry buoyed by the optimism of her beloved sister, Lynn. Although Lynn's untimely death renders her heartbroken, Katie musters self-reliance and in turn becomes an inspiration to others. Her entire family honors Lynn's legacy, reminding readers to cherish glittering hope, even in the toughest of times.

5. Cassie from the *Roll of Thunder, Hear My Cry* saga by Mildred D. Taylor

The Logans cling to their land and little victories amidst poverty and prejudice in 1930s Mississippi. Although Mama strives to shield her children from the pain of racism, Cassie grows up fast as the seeds of the Civil Rights Movement are planted in her family farm. Students will grapple right along with the characters in the hard choices between when to stand down and when to stand up for yourself.

6. Stanley from *Holes* and Armpit from *Small Steps* by Louis Sachar

Sentenced to hard labor for a crime he didn't commit, Stanley digs deep into a family curse that turns to fortune. This intricate, ingenious tale of friendship and fortitude will provoke debate about how much control we have over fate. Both books' memorable multicultural characters embody the pluck and persistence of a growth mindset.

7. Meg from the *A Wrinkle in Time* books by Madeline L'Engle

Swept into a strange, scary new dimension on a desperate search to save her father and baby brother, Meg summons the supremacy of love to win the day. Alternately harrowing and heartwarming, readers discover the only way to defeat darkness is with the light inside us all.

8. Marty from the *Shiloh* quartet of books by Phyllis Reynolds Naylor

In these deceptively simple books, Marty discovers the ramifications of lying, the meaning of love, and the lesson that everyone deserves a second chance. Ultimately, the theme of revenge is turned on its head as a reviled man, who was severely abused as a child, learns that pay back isn't always an eye for an eye but can instead be a kindness for a kindness.

9. Bradley from *There's a Boy in the Girls' Bathroom* by Louis Sachar

A schoolyard bully's life is forever changed when a new student and new counselor refuse to let him push them away. That is, until they both betray him and break his heart. Black eyes may heal, but can Bradley put his heart back together again all by himself? One of the funniest, wisest, and most touching of all the books my students read, I cannot recommend this book more highly.

Expanding the Literary Canon

The measure of greatness or worth of a novel doesn't come from its particularities of plot, author, or narrator but from its universalities of artistry, imagination, empathy, inclusion, equity, and altruism. As long as a book's overriding message is one of unity and love, it deserves to read and cherished.

Instead of arguing about why this or that book doesn't meet your students' needs or your notion of correctness, let's agree to disagree, respect each other's choices, and move forward together in extolling the virtues of our individual favorite novels, both old and newly discovered. True book lovers are always hungry for book recommendations, so do your part to create more classics and to expand the literary canon.

More voices! More reading! More discussions! More books!

Chapter 3.
Teaching Film as Literature

As I explain in my article for KQED's *In the Classroom* blog (2018), I currently teach English language arts at a film and media magnet middle school in East Hollywood, CA. The main novels my 8th graders read together in my class are *Roll of Thunder, Hear My Cry* and *The Watsons Go to Birmingham—1963*.

Because both works of fiction feature actual events that occur during historical periods largely unfamiliar to most middle school students—the Great Depression of the 1930s, sharecropping, segregation, the Civil Rights Movement, and the 1963 Birmingham church bombings—I must provide ongoing historical background so my students can comprehend and make inferences about these stories.

One way I accomplish this historical context is through the use of film. However, the movies I use not only augment my students' understanding of these great books; the films I show can also stand alone as worthy works of art and literature to both learn from and appreciate (Davis, 2013). In this way, media becomes an integral part of my ELA curriculum and instruction.

Recommended Historical Films

Both ELA and history teachers can use the following movies as the basis for lively discussions, essays, and projects related to the themes and issues explored in these fine films. Each one of these movies is a triumph in acting, directing, and storytelling. Viewed in the following order, students gain a broad historical overview, especially concerning the African-American experience.

1. ***The Adventures of Huck Finn*** (Disney, 1993, rated PG)

Set in the South during the 1830s, a young boy learns the consequences of lying, the meaning of loyalty, and the importance of liberty for all, as he helps a runaway slave escape along the mighty Mississippi River.

2. *Seabiscuit* (Universal/DreamWorks, 2003, rated PG-13)

Set before and during the Great Depression, this incredible, inspirational true tale about a jockey, a trainer, an owner, and a horse, all who literally beat the odds, will have students alternately cheering and weeping.

3. *The Untold Story of Emmett Louis Till* (Velocity, 2006, rated PG-13)

Director Keith Beauchamp's acclaimed and influential documentary about the torture and lynching of a Northern black boy, who dared to whistle at a white woman in 1955 Mississippi, convinced the U.S. Justice Department to reopen the case nearly 50 years later.

4. *The Long Walk Home* (Dave Bell/New Visions, 1990, rated PG)

Set in 1955 in Alabama, a white privileged housewife eventually breaks with her family and friends to support her black maid's participation in the Montgomery bus boycott.

5. *Ruby Bridges* (Disney, 1998, rated TV-PG)

Set in 1960 in New Orleans, an exceptionally bright first grade girl breaks a color barrier and teaches her family and community a lesson in fortitude and forgiveness that is utterly unforgettable.

6. *Sins of the Father* (FX, 2002, no rating: language, adult situations, violence)

Alternating between the past and the present, this film features a determined FBI agent and a now-grown-up, conflicted boy, who ensure that justice is served some thirty years after four little girls were murdered.

7. *Guess Who's Coming to Dinner?* (Columbia Pictures, 1967, not rated)

Set in San Francisco in 1967, a liberal couple's convictions and long marriage are put to the test when their daughter and her fiancé teach two sets of parents the glory of love.

Preparing to Teach Films

Parent Permission: At the beginning of every school year, it's wise to get parent pre-permission for all of the movies you plan to show to your students. Consult your school district's policy for showing films, and send home a letter for parents to sign and return that outlines the movies you intend to show this year, including each movie's MPAA rating and its instructional merit.

Character List: Look up the cast list for all movies on *IMDb*. Compile a list of the major characters in a movie, giving students the first and last name along with a brief explanation of who each character is.

During the Movie

A Communal Experience: Just as I always prefer to have whole-class novels read entirely while in class, I want the viewing of movies to be a communal experience. We aren't merely studying these films; my students are collectively living these journeys with the characters in real time. I do not flip the learning of movies by having my students view them beforehand at home. I want us gasping, laughing, and sobbing as one!

Note Taking: I require my students to take notes during every movie, with half a page in their notebooks devoted to each important character. I keep enough light on in the room so students can see what they write. Since I don't want students watching two screens at one time, these notes are always written in their notebooks. This way, if students later compose their essays on a computer, they can easily access their handwritten notes.

Depending on the topic of the upcoming essay, students document relevant evidence from the movie beside the appropriate character's name. Students are responsible for their own notes, but I do pause the movie at important junctures to ask questions, conduct short discussions, and clarify confusions.

Honoring the Art: Even though I pause each movie several times, I do so judiciously and only when it doesn't interfere with the flow of the plot. Clarifications and conversations may be necessary at certain points, but I always wait until the arc of the current action has subsided. This policy also holds true for when I choose to stop the reading of class novels in order to discuss the finer aspects of the work.

A Multitude of Sources

By adding narrative and documentary films to my repertoire of historical sources and class novels, I provide my students with a varied learning experience that goes beyond the printed page, requiring them to listen carefully and watch attentively. In this way, my students become increasingly savvy and sophisticated in their interactions with media.

Many of the activities and literary devices explained in the next chapters are applicable to movies, and I routinely discuss things like foreshadowing, irony, themes, and symbolism while we view films.

Film Versions of Novels

Since many beloved books have been made into movies, I inform my students when a novel we're about to read together has a film version. I tell them that we absolutely will see the movie together, but only after we've read the entire book as a class. In the meantime, I ask for their patience. Just like I tell them not to read ahead in the novel we're reading, I ask my students to also promise not to watch the film version—not to watch it if it comes on TV and not to rent, buy, download, or stream it—before we see it together.

Similarly, if a student happens to have already read the novel we're going to read as a class or has already seen its film version, I ask them for their discretion in not discussing with their classmates what's to come in the plot. I'm dead serious about students not ruining any surprises or outcomes of any books they've read previously. I also tell them that they haven't read this book *with me* and that I'm going to count on them to be able to read between the lines and make inferences better than those who are reading the book for the first time. Having already read an upcoming whole-class novel makes a student's task harder, not easier, as I expect much more from these students. (And I'm always thrilled when these students later tell me they never loved and got so much out of the book they'd read before as much as while reading it with me!)

Comparing and contrasting a movie with its filmed version is a fun and informative way to further analyze a book. One way I have my students take notes during the film version of a novel we've just completed is for them to list all the character and plot changes they identify in the movie. We then can discuss and they can write about the possible reasons why these changes were made, as well as analyze the merits of these switches, additions, and deletions.

Chapter 4.

The Reader's Notebook

I've created a wonderful system for teaching whole-class novels that allows my students to document their rich reading and writing experiences and to interact with text on a deep level. My reader's notebooks serve as my students' portfolios for their growth in literacy and their path to becoming lifelong readers (Ripp, 2018).

Here are the main components of my reader's notebooks:

1. Table of Contents
2. Works Cited/MLA Format
3. Vocabulary
4. Settings
5. Characters
6. Figurative Language
    a. Simile
    b. Metaphor
    c. Hyperbole
    d. Idiom
    e. Alliteration
7. Citations
8. Literary Devices
    a. Symbols
    b. Irony
    c. Foreshadowing
    d. Themes
9. Predictions
10. Taking a Stand

It's important to know that except for the table of contents, every component listed above is written separately for every book we read together within the same reader's notebook. Since we read at least six major and minor whole-class novels, there's a separate vocabulary, settings, character, etc. section in the reader's notebook for all the books we read together. My students constantly refer to the notes about our previous novels, as they compare and contrast each succeeding novel we read together.

Here are a few basic guidelines for my reader's notebooks, along with my rationales for why I've chosen these procedures:

Composition books are used for reader's notebooks.

Old-school composition books are inexpensive and readily available. Standard 100-sheet, 200-page, 9 ¾" x 7 ½" composition books are the perfect size for a wealth of notes. With this smaller-sized notebook, classroom storage space is kept to a minimum, and there's more elbow room for collaborative work. Also, the composition books' hardboard covers provide a sturdy writing surface.

Students keep their reader's notebooks in class at all times.

Every class period, these notebooks are passed out and collected by student monitors. This ensures that every student is prepared each day, and teachers never have to deal with lost or forgotten notebooks.

Students write only with pencil in these notebooks.

With pencils, mistakes are easily erased, and mechanical pencils keep writing neat. Since we use all 200 pages, students must not tear out any pages. Severe student mistakes are mitigated by the teacher on a case-by-case basis, and I ask my students to alert me whenever they're tempted to tear out a page of their notebook.

These notebooks are only for serious, neat, professional English class work.

Doodling and decorating are not components of these reader's notebooks. Students already are invited to be artistic when they illustrate their original book covers for their Book Jacket Reports (explained in Chapter 8). These notebooks are personalized by the originality and insight of the notes and writing contained within the covers, rather than by creating "ownership" with ornamentation that isn't connected to their reading.

Students pre-number all 200 pages.

Having every page numbered beforehand makes it very easy to keep these notebooks organized and cohesive. Most often, the left-hand, even-numbered pages are reserved for examples, and the right-hand, odd-numbered pages are for corresponding textual evidence.

Here are explanations of my reader's notebook components:

Table of Contents

As I add different components to different books, the students update their table of contents for their reader's notebooks.

Works Cited/MLA Format

Here we list the books that we read as a class, written in proper MLA format. The MLA format procedures are also written here for future student reference.

Vocabulary

On my own, I thoroughly preview all books we read as a class and compile a list of the words that likely will be unfamiliar to my students. I mostly include those words that reoccur several times throughout the book, rather than focusing on random words that only occur once (Kwedor, 2019). Of course, if certain isolated words are crucial to the understanding of the plot or historical context of a novel, those words are also included in my vocabulary list.

Here are some examples of important vocabulary words that occur in *Roll of Thunder, Hear My Cry*: *grumble, grouse, gripe; haste; flounce; smirk; goad; Union, Yankee; Confederate, Rebel; acre; cotton gin; mortgage note; property taxes; boycott; gully; gaze.*

Before beginning a new novel, my students copy all vocabulary words from my master list into their reader's notebooks. They write these words only on the left-hand pages of the vocabulary sections of their notebooks.

Before we read a new part of the novel, I preview the words that will be seen in today's reading and define any brand-new words. For each of the words we've seen and discussed before, I provide a simple definition and call on students for the correct corresponding vocabulary word.

In the vocabulary sections of the reader's notebooks, the right-hand pages are reserved for the page number evidence of each vocabulary word and headed as *Vocabulary Evidence*. After a student has provided the correct matching vocabulary word for my definition, I say the page number/s of where the word will occur in today's reading, and the students write these page numbers in their notebooks. As time goes by, students can clearly see by the amount of page number evidence for each word how important these words are to their comprehension of the story. With these regular vocabulary previews, every student is prepared to fully comprehend each day's reading.

For subsequent novels we read together, I create a new vocabulary list. I include on that new vocabulary list any previous vocabulary words from past novels we've read that also occur in our new book. I want my students to see how ubiquitous these words are and therefore how important it is to know their meanings.

Here are some examples of common vocabulary words that occur frequently in many young adult novels: *mumble, mutter, murmur; flabbergasted, dumbfounded, dumbstruck, awestruck; tremble, quiver, quaver; reluctant; hesitate; puzzle, bewilder, baffle, befuddle; glisten, glitter, glint, gleam; aloof; wince, flinch, cringe; mourn, grieve.*

Settings

On the left-hand side of the reader's notebook, settings are listed under this heading:

Preposition + Major Settings: Time and Place, When and Where

The most important times and places are listed and always preceded by a preposition. We discuss the proper use of prepositions (most commonly, *at, in,* or *on*) and, when applicable, we include settings such as: year, historical period, region, city, state, month, season, etc.

In the settings sections, the right side of the notebook is reserved for *Setting Evidence*. Here we list the page numbers or chapters in which each setting was found.

After we read, we first discuss any old settings that were revisited in our day's reading of the book and document the corresponding new pages/chapters. Then we discuss and list any new settings we found in the day's reading, along with the pages/chapters.

Here are some examples of major settings for *The Watsons Go to Birmingham—1963*:

- Historical Period: during the Civil Rights Movement
- on the school bus
- in the upstairs bathroom
- under the green apple tree in the alley behind Mitchell's
- at a rest stop in Ohio
- Region: in the deep South
- at Collier's Landing

Characters

On the left-hand side of the notebook, characters are listed under this heading:

Important Characters, Appositives, and Page Number First Seen

After discussing any old or new settings for the day's reading (see above), we discuss and note page numbers or chapters for any old characters who reappeared in the book today. This page number/chapter evidence goes on the corresponding right-hand pages headed as *Character Evidence*. Then we list any new characters introduced in the day's reading, along with the page number where each character first appeared.

Characters are listed with their first and last names, followed by a comma and an appositive that gives relevant information about who this character is and/or how they relate to other characters. These relationships are a great way to teach and reinforce the use of apostrophes to show possession or ownership, such as: *Darry Curtis, Ponyboy's oldest brother*. For books that contain a multitude of important characters, these lists greatly assist reading comprehension.

Here are some examples of important characters for *Shiloh*:

- Marty Preston, the eleven-year-old narrator who rescues Shiloh
- Judd Travers, Shiloh's abusive owner
- Mr. Wallace, the owner of the store in town
- David Howard, Marty's best friend
- Baker's German Shepherd, the dog that always gets loose and that attacked Shiloh

Figurative Language

Students take the following four notes on the *Figurative Language* page of their reader's notebooks:

1. The use of figurative language is the way an author acts more like an artist or a poet by adding creative and original words to their story in order to make their writing more interesting and alive.
2. Literal language is when the words mean *exactly* what they say.
3. Figurative language is when the words mean something *other* than what they say.
4. Examples of figurative language: simile, metaphor, hyperbole, idiom, alliteration

For each whole-class novel, I devote at least a page in the reader's notebook for each of the following five examples of figurative language:

- **Simile:** comparing two unlike things using *like, as,* or *than*
- **Metaphor:** directly comparing two unlike things that share some common characteristics
- **Hyperbole:** an extreme exaggeration
- **Idiom:** a common expression meaning something other than what the words say
- **Alliteration:** the purposeful repeating of the same starting letter or sound
    - Here are some examples of alliteration from *The Watson Go to Birmingham—1963:* Weird Watsons, Brown Bomber, Cockeye Kenny, Genesee Junkyard

After we discuss settings and characters, students are asked to identify evidence from the book for the specific examples of figurative language on the pages I give them. I preselect a few of the clearest and most necessary examples of figurative language for each day's reading. By the end of a novel, I've balanced the total number of pieces of evidence for each of the five examples of figurative language that occur in the book.

The textual evidence for any example of figurative language I ask the students to identify is written in the form of a citation. This is a way I can regularly reinforce and students can practice writing proper citations.

Citations

I spent years teaching my students how to write citations properly. Correctly copying from a text can be quite confusing and is full of different instances where new procedures must be added. Yet there just had to be a simpler, clearer way to teach my middle schoolers how cite textual evidence with confidence (Jody and Shara, 2015). I finally realized that if they could master the use of and the occasion for a just few pesky punctuation marks, my students would have a strong foundation in correctly citing textual evidence.

But how to clarify the placement of those wily ellipsis, periods, parenthesis, and double and single quotation marks? I decided to chunk these punctuation marks, and I devised a simple set of five questions in a specific order that students can ask themselves when citing from a text.

My students write the following five questions in their reader's notebooks:

1. What is necessary to copy?

Appropriate, accurate, and adequate evidence is essential! Copy only as much of the text as you need in order to clearly present your evidence. Then use double quotation marks to show where you started and stopped copying: "_____" Copy one to a maximum of four sentences from the text per citation.

2. Did I cut out any unnecessary, irrelevant words or sentences?

If so, use ellipsis to show where you cut out words or sentences that were not necessary or relevant to your evidence—at the beginning, middle, and/or end of what you copied: …

3. Is any character speaking out loud to another character using dialogue?

If so, use single quotation marks to show where a character started and stopped speaking within your citation: '_____'

4. What author and page did I copy from?

Use parenthesis around the author's last name and page number and place the period <u>after</u> the parenthesis: (Author, page number).

5. How should I introduce my citation?

Choose one of the introductions below to begin your citation:

- According to the text,
- As stated in the text,
- According to the author,
- As the author states,

When beginning a citation that includes dialogue, introduce the character who is speaking:

- As _____ said, " '
- As _____ said to _____, " '
- As _____ told _____, " '

***

Suddenly, something complex was broken down into a few easily understandable parts. I know all my students will master this skill eventually because it's a process we regularly practice together step by step. When we want to write a citation, I call on five students to answer one of the five citation questions. Once we have all the information we need, the students individually write their correct citation in their notebooks. (I, of course, model this on the board the first several times.)

Next, I call on yet another student and say, "Using words like *comma, double quotation mark, single quotation mark, ellipsis, parenthesis,* and *period*, please read us your citation including all the punctuation marks." As the student reads aloud, I interject what each punctuation mark means: "Double quotation marks mean you started copying… A single quotation mark means a character started speaking… Ellipsis cut out words…"

By second semester, the scaffolds come down. I call on double the number of students as I now ask *them* tell me what each succeeding citation question is, and then I call on yet another student to answer each of those questions. By the end of the year, every student has this process committed to memory! And it never gets boring because the content they're citing is always new. This skill is also independently applied each time my students write an essay that requires textual evidence.

Here are some examples of figurative language written in the form of a citation by some of the authors featured in Chapter 2:

- **Simile:** According to the text, "It was hot as a furnace in the house…" (Curtis, p. 190).

- **Metaphor:** As the author states, "… A gigantic coon… baked in a sea of onions, garlic, and fat orange-yellow yams…" (Taylor, p. 123).

- **Hyperbole:** Judd warned Marty, " 'But he does somethin' I don't like, I kick him clear to China' " (Naylor, p. 55).

- **Idiom:** "A chip off the block" means a person is just like their parent (Hinton, p. 48).

***

The final three components of the reader's notebook (literary devices, prediction, and taking a stand), will be explained in the next chapter.

Chapter 5.
Literary Devices, Predictions, and Taking a Stand

I regularly teach whole-class novels to guide my students beyond a surface reading of great books and toward a deeper understanding of the author's use of literary devices—particularly, symbolism, irony, foreshadowing, and themes. Although symbols can be difficult for young readers to grasp, the quest to decipher their meanings can actually become empowering and compelling.

Literary Symbols: A Reading Treasure Hunt

While I also teach simile, metaphor, hyperbole, idiom, and alliteration, I don't teach symbolism merely as a figure of speech (for example, "a new dawn"). I'm more interested in helping my students discover and interpret the symbolic additions to the story that authors cleverly employ to convey important messages.

I tell my students that the best way to identify potential literary symbols is to watch for aspects of the book that seem unnecessary. In fact, if you removed a symbol from the book, this deletion wouldn't change the main story at all. Although a symbol sometimes is engaging or amusing, the fact remains that its literal information is essentially extraneous.

The question then becomes: *Why would an author interrupt the dramatic action to include superfluous details or story elements, even those that may add a small amount of interest or humor?*

The astonishing answer is that a skillful author never wastes the reader's time because every detail has been carefully considered. All symbols are inserted strategically and won't work as well, or even at all, if placed somewhere else in the story. Therefore, a true symbol isn't irrelevant but actually adds depth to an already-entertaining book.

Here's the graphic organizer I created to help my students understand symbols, along with examples from some of the books we read together:

Symbol	Stands for, represents, signifies, means	Book title
Identify/Find	Infer/Figure out	Page number
Mr. Robert, Toddy the dog, and Joe Louis have all lost the urge to fight or hunt.	This represents Byron's sudden change for the better. By decides not to fight Grandma Sands and actually enjoys fishing and hanging out with the men in Birmingham.	*The Watsons Go to Birmingham—1963* (page 163)
Marty twice mentioned seeing the fox with a gray body and red head.	This means we're all products of our parents. Judd Travers is physically cruel to his dogs, just as his dad was abusive with him.	*Shiloh* (page 3 and 58)
Mama allowed a strand of her hair to fall and remain, but Papa pushed the hair back in place.	This stands for the heavy price Mama had to pay for standing up to the Wallace brothers and how she now wants to give up. However, Papa's unspoken message to her is to persevere.	*Roll of Thunder, Hear My Cry* (page 157)
Two-Bit scraped the egg off of the kitchen clock.	This represents the time the Curtis brothers have to stay together and how it's ticking away.	*The Outsiders* (page 108)
Bradley sat on a torn red couch in the barbershop.	This signifies how Bradley's heart has been ripped apart by Carla leaving.	*There's a Boy in the Girls' Bathroom* (page 168)

Symbolism mustn't be confused with foreshadowing. Symbols inform what has already happened or what's happening now in the story but never indicate what's to come. Carefully analyzing the scene in which the symbol occurs or reflecting on what's happened recently in the plot assists students in figuring out a symbol's meaning.

Of course, authors don't provide a symbols code book, so it's up to the reader to suss out viable interpretations for each potential symbol. While some explanations of a symbol's meaning may be perfectly logical, I remind students that their inferences ultimately must jibe with the overarching themes of the book.

For example, students often misinterpret the first example in the template above from *The Watsons Go to Birmingham—1963*. They often assume this symbol signifies that the Southern blacks are weary of the struggle for civil rights and want to give up. However, this definitely isn't the message the author wants to impart.

After we've successfully figured out a symbol's meaning, I ask the class, "Do you think we're reading too much into this? Are we just making this up? Are we certain the author intended us to discover this symbol and to interpret it in this way?"

My band of literary scholars always answers with confident affirmation!

I also underscore that most young adult authors respect the reader's intelligence so much they're willing to add symbols to their books, even though these hidden gems of meaning and wisdom largely go unnoticed by students and teachers alike. Nevertheless, these authors are counting on their young audiences to read carefully and to read between the lines so they enjoy a rich and rewarding literary experience.

With initial modeling and guided instruction, pairs of students are eventually able to collaborate on finding and figuring out the symbols in the novel we're reading. To scaffold this assignment, I provide my students with the page numbers on which symbols appear. I circulate through the room to listen in on their engrossed conversations and to offer support and praise. My students take their detective work seriously, and their frequent high fives as they successfully puzzle out a symbol's meaning are a delight to witness.

Irony

In the reader's notebook, evidence of irony is documented under this heading:

Irony: An Unexpected, Strangely Funny Effect

Like symbols, irony can be a tricky concept for students to understand; but with practice, my students appreciate this subtle and sophisticated literary device.

Here are some ironic incidents from a couple of the whole-class books my students often read:

From *The Watsons Go to Birmingham—1963*:

- It is ironic that Kenny thought Rufus would save him by being far away from him. This is unexpected yet strangely funny because Rufus actually saved Kenny by becoming his close friend.

From *The Outsiders*:

- It is ironic that Darry said he "didn't mean to" slap Ponyboy. This is unexpected yet strangely funny because Darry had just mocked Pony for saying that he "didn't mean to" fall asleep in the vacant lot.

- It is ironic that Ponyboy fantasized about running away to the country. This is unexpected yet strangely funny because Pony's dream has become a living nightmare while he and Johnny hide out from the police in the country.

- It is ironic that Pony and Johnny use Johnny's switchblade to painfully cut each other's long hair, which is the worst thing you can do to a greaser. This is strangely funny because it was with that same knife that Johnny killed Bob, and it's unexpected because the very weapon that was supposed to protect them actually got Johnny and Pony into all this trouble.

As will be explained in this chapter, we don't talk about irony or symbols again until the next time we see them occur in one of our whole-class novels. Also, with modeling and scaffolding, I always allow my students to determine meaning for themselves without me merely telling them what they should know.

Using the first two irony examples above, I would facilitate a class discussion by asking:

- "Who can tell us what was ironic—what was unexpected yet strangely funny—about Kenny thinking Rufus would save him by being as far away from him as possible?"

- "Explain to us the irony—the unexpected but strangely funny effect—of Darry saying that he 'didn't mean to' slap Ponyboy."

Foreshadowing

In the reader's notebook, evidence of foreshadowing is written under the heading:

Foreshadowing: Hints or clues for what will happen later in the story

Evidence of foreshadowing proves to students that writing is a very precise craft. Authors don't haphazardly piece together a plot; they work diligently to create a story that shows planning and ingenuity (Potter, 2016). I also explain that authors don't necessarily expect the reader to spot foreshadowing in the moment. However, authors do hope that when what's been hinted at is finally revealed, the reader will pause and think, *Wasn't that hinted at before?* Careful readers will often flip back in the book to locate the instances where clues were given by the author.

When seeking evidence of foreshadowing, I ask my students, "Did we know this was going to happen?" When they often reply, "No," I say something like, "Well, let's go back about fifty pages. What do you see on page ___ that subtly warned us this would occur?"

Here's some evidence of foreshadowing in the books we read:

From *The Outsiders*:

- Ponyboy wondering what it would be like inside a burning cigarette ember foreshadowed Pony and Johnny rushing into the burning church to save the schoolchildren.

From *Shiloh*:

- When Marty mentions to Dad and Judd Travers that he hasn't seen any dog in the yard, just that German Shepherd of Baker's that gets loose sometimes, this foreshadowed Shiloh getting attacked by that same dog.

(The last literary device of the reader's notebooks, themes, will be explained in Chapter 7.)

Predictions: Activating Curiosity and Honoring Student Input

Predicting is a wonderful engagement tool because it encourages your students to be wonder-filled! The act of predicting places students in the driver's seat of learning as they step into the author's shoes to guess what's to come.

Allow your students to be forward thinking and to come up with their own predictions based on these three qualities:

1. A prediction is an educated guess, not a random assumption.
2. Make informed predictions based on your personal prior knowledge or on what has been previously read, rather than making wild guesses that have little basis in facts or probability.
3. Good predictions are based on logic, reason, and thinking and can always be supported with a clear explanation.

Invite your students to use their own intelligence and imagination to speculate about what probably will occur next (or soon) in the book. This seemingly small challenge empowers students to become active participants in the reading process and gives them a stake in the story.

Accurately predicting what will happen next in a well-crafted novel often is met with red herrings and surprises, but these startling twists and turns are actually what make stories so fascinating. Therefore, prepare your students to expect that while reading stories, their predictions frequently will be wrong—and that this is part of the fun! Calling a book or movie "predictable" is no compliment, but it sure is worth it to try to outguess the author.

Predict Privately

Initially, have your students keep their predictions, both written and imagined, to themselves in order to preserve the collective mystery of what may happen next. Also, always have students add an explanation as to why they think this will happen. Do not have students share their predictions aloud with the class. You don't want a student who happens to know for sure what will happen next or one who has predicted correctly all on their own spoiling things for everyone else.

The prediction section of the reader's notebook contains the heading:

My Predictions: Educated Guesses

Here are some important predictions my students make for the following books. Notice how these prediction writing prompts require an explanation:

From *The Watsons Go to Birmingham—1963*:

- I think that after killing the bird, Byron will/will not change for the better because…

- After the church bombing, I think Kenny will react by…

From *Roll of Thunder, Hear My Cry*:

- I think the seven cars of nightriders suddenly left the Logan farm because…

- I think Papa's advice to Cassie about getting revenge on Lillian Jean will be…

Revisit Prior Predictions

When you ask your students to write down their predictions, always double back at a later date and have them silently reread their original prediction for what they have just seen revealed. This way, students can formally confirm if they had predicted correctly or incorrectly.

If it was important to have students actually write down a prediction, then it's all the more important for them to revisit it later. For those insightful students who got it right and are boasting about their foresight, you can now ask a few of them to read aloud what they had previously written. This provides evidence of their correct prediction, as well as the reasoning behind it that led them to this correct supposition. This explicit demonstration of the thinking process allows developing students to see into another student's method of logic and deduction.

Use Suspense to Your Advantage

One way to keep your class fresh and fascinating is to create suspense. Creating anticipation for tomorrow's lesson goes a long way in keeping your students involved—and in attendance! Cliffhangers are built into most books, especially at the end of a chapter. Use these junctures in the plot to decide where to pause the day's reading and to ask your students to make a prediction.

The Whole-Child Benefits of Practicing Forward Thinking

When kids train their minds to think beyond the present, to read between the lines, and to connect the dots in a logical fashion, they develop the habit of being proactive. Thinking ahead in all aspects of life increases your awareness in the present and develops mindfulness. It also allows you to prepare for the future.

Think about it: Unless you are keenly aware of what's happening now, as well as what happened before, how can you accurately guess what will come? The act of predicting activates a presence of mind that's perfectly suited to the learning process.

This sense of foresight goes a long way in preventing a person from being reactive and becoming stressed out when life presents them with a challenge or obstacle they really could've seen coming had they thought just a little bit ahead. Life is full of unpredictable curveballs and changes that may add anguish and frustration to our days; but to a large degree, a forward-thinking person can mitigate and often circumvent altogether many of the disasters that others spend too much time dealing with and fretting over.

Also, when we talk about developing students' social skills, teaching kids to be considerate tops our list. And what is consideration but anticipating and attending to the needs of others?

Taking a Stand: Engaging Students through Controversy

Push your students' buttons from time to time! Provoke them and rile them up!

But do so within a set of established procedures so students can air their thoughtful, informed opinions in a civil and intelligent manner. Honoring your students' ideas and insights is a great way to get them "into" a new lesson or to reinvigorate them when their interest wanes.

Offer up a polemic related to what your students are currently studying or reading and require them to take and defend a stand. Students spontaneously respond to pointed, provocative comments and ideas. They love to add their two cents, particularly where issues of justice, equity, and freedom are concerned. Just be sure to elevate your students' intense reactions, especially when those responses are knee-jerk and uninformed, to eloquent expressions of perspective and passion. Teach respectful debate skills and awaken in your students the fire of self-expression.

The controversial issue's connection to your current instructional topic doesn't even have to be explicated beforehand. When you stir up controversy, your students won't care how it's related to what they've been or will study; they just want to chime in! Students are always thrilled when someone welcomes and values their points of view. If the underlying purpose doesn't become apparent until later, its revelation will only be more impactful when you once again prove how all learning in your class is interconnected and personally relevant.

Pros and Cons

Ethical dilemmas, controversy, and topics for debate are always available to the teacher who's perceptive and interested in the profound. Keenly look for opportunities for your students to air their opinions about thorny issues and questionable predicaments related to your curriculum. Since controversy is a natural motivator, use children's innate quests for fairness and self-determination, as you open their eyes to abuse, oppression, and bias—throughout history, across the globe, and in their own communities.

According to Jennifer Rich (2018), "Inclusive classrooms… allow for uncomfortable conversations where close examinations of… crises of social justice can be debated in thoughtful ways. Even young children can—and should—learn to 'raise their collective voices.' It is reasonable to expect disagreement, but it is essential to provide opportunities for students to learn how to have difficult conversations respectfully."

Taking a Stand

A wonderful way to infuse debate into your lessons is with my Taking a Stand activity. This engaging strategy works for many reasons:

- It's a quick process,
- it teaches students to commit to a decision,
- it gets students out of their seats,
- it gives students a respectful forum to present their opinions,
- it allows students to change their opinions later, and
- it lays a foundation for more formal argumentative/persuasive essays or debates.

Simply have your students make a sort of T-Chart in their reader's notebooks. On the left-hand page, they write the following heading: *Agree, Pro, For, True, Believe, Correct/Right, Support,* and they draw both a plus/positive symbol and a thumbs-up.

On the right-hand page, the heading is: *Disagree, Con, Against, False, Disbelieve, Incorrect/Wrong, Oppose,* and they draw a minus/negative symbol and a thumbs-down. Students now have a template onto which they can routinely write their opinions concerning the various issues you present to them through the year.

Using as many synonyms as possible, both when they're taking notes or when you're talking to them, constantly suffuses students with academic language that's readily understandable in the moment. This is one organic way you can meet the requirements of English Language Development (ELD) standards.

Getting Kids to Commit

During the Taking a Stand activity, always emphasize that students must take a stand either way. There's no middle ground here, and no equivocation is allowed. Life is full of grey areas, but wishy-washiness is never a hallmark of good writing or speaking.

Besides, you'll teach students how to address and counter opposing opinions at other junctures throughout the year (see Chapter 11). For this activity, however, students must only write on one page on one side of their notebook (pro or con) and take a clear stand for each issue you present to them.

For an example with a narrative text, such as *The Outsiders*, you could propose the following dilemma: "Randy the Soc is thinking about not fighting in tonight's rumble. In your opinion, explain the wisest choice for Randy to make regarding the big fight. You may use evidence from the book and your own ideas to support your opinion."

Then give your students a choice between two sentence starters to guide their opinions. They're either "for" or "against" Randy fighting in the rumble, so they only write on the left- or right-hand page in the Taking a Stand section of their notebooks.

Students either begin with *"Randy should fight in the rumble because…"* or *"Randy should not fight in the rumble because…"* Notice that each sentence starter has a "because" built into it so students are forced to explain their opinions using a complete sentence. Tell students they can believe whatever they choose but must always explain why they believe so. Requiring students to write down their opinions forces them to be more thoughtful and articulate and also ensures they actually commit to a response.

Literally Taking a Stand

After giving your students a few minutes to write down their responses and explanations, direct their attention to the aisles on each side of the classroom. The left aisle is for those who are "for" the issue at hand, and the right aisle is for those who are "against" it.

Proactively manage this passage with firm, clear instructions: Students are to take their reader's notebooks with them as they silently move to the aisle that corresponds with the response they just wrote. They're to stand shoulder to shoulder with whichever classmates are on the same side of the room as they are. You want to see all their faces, so be sure no one is behind anyone else.

Also, emphasize that we're treating each other's opinions with respect. Even if there are only a few people, or even a single student, standing on one side of the room, that shouldn't engender any giggles or ridicule. After doing this activity a few times, this procedure will flow smoothly; but don't rush into out-of-seat activities like this until your classroom management has been well established!

The reason why this activity works so well, especially with middle schoolers, is because it forces them to commit. Asking students to simply raise their hand while you take a quick poll often is a waste of time because adolescents can be extremely self-conscious about standing out and so consumed with fitting in that even the most innocuous question gets kids raising their hands *only if* their friends are also already doing so. It's impossible to gauge where students stand on anything when half of them are too timid or lazy to even raise their hand at all.

During Taking a Stand, if you see a student begin to walk to one side of the room and suddenly shift to other side where their friends happen to be or where most of the class is, rush over and check their notebook to see exactly on which side they had written their response. That's where you'll ask the student be true to their convictions and take their stand, even if they're standing alone.

Reading Their Responses Aloud

Next, ask for volunteers or call on students to read their responses aloud. Of course, all students respectfully and attentively listen to each other read their responses. Be sure to hear a sampling of responses from both sides.

When responding, require all students to read their sentences aloud from their notebooks. They're not allowed to extemporize unless you ask them follow-up questions. This is important because you want to train students to write cogent thoughts and explanations the first time without merely relying on ad-libbing their responses later. Students often have plenty of intelligent thoughts but sometimes are too lazy to actually write them down in a coherent manner. This activity will fix that.

The teacher always stands in the middle of the room during this process so the students don't know where you personally stand on the issue at hand. With experience with the same issues, you'll already know where most students will initially stand, and it's often on the wrong side. Yet you will lead them down the garden path anyway because this is probably just where you or the author expects students' initial, uninformed opinions to be at this point. Don't worry if students have misconceptions and prejudices at the beginning because once you fully explore each issue, it'll become quite clear to the entire class where evidence and reason will prevail.

The Option to Reconsider

The beauty of Taking a Stand is that you always allow your students to reconsider once they've heard a variety of their peers' opposing responses. Once both sides have aired their perspectives, allow a moment for students to change their minds and to show this shift in opinion by physically changing sides.

This is a powerful moment when students learn how a wealth of facts and explanations allows us to make an informed decision and to possibly reconsider our initial responses. This option to reconsider and to physically change sides is one that can be revisited later as many times as necessary as more evidence is added to each side's case.

Here are some more examples of how I ask my students to take a stand.

From *The Outsiders*:

- Carrying the switchblade ended up helping *or* hurting Johnny because…

- Had there been no fire in the church, Dallas would have advised Johnny to turn himself in *or* to remain in hiding because…

From *Shiloh*:

- In order to be a truly humane person, you should *or* should not become a vegetarian or vegan because…

- It is appropriate *or* not appropriate for an eleven-year-old to own their own rifle because…

Placing Everything in Context Organically

I don't teach anything in abstract or isolation. I only teach the literary concepts I've already planned to focus upon, and I teach those concepts only when they occur *organically* in the novels my students will be studying. You can fill your own reader's notebooks with any ELA content standards you choose, adding to or adjusting what I've suggested in this and the previous chapter. Just be sure the concepts you select do indeed occur, and occur frequently, in the novels you will be teaching.

For example, any vocabulary words you hold your students accountable for should be academic vocabulary words you constantly use in class or words that are integral to the text you're currently studying. Don't make up random lists for your students to memorize, no matter how "important" those words may ostensibly be. Import always comes from necessity and frequency because this is how students truly learn and retain vocabulary, not from mere memorizing.

Likewise, don't teach any examples of figurative language or literary devices until they occur organically in a text. I don't teach something like irony until the time there's actually evidence of irony in the book we're currently reading. If there's no more evidence of irony for the next fifty pages, then it's not discussed until it reappears.

Building Trust

On the first day of school, I explicitly tell my students that *everything* we talk about and learn in this class will be repeated several times throughout the year. It may come up again in five minutes, tomorrow, next week, in two months, or not until next semester—but reoccur it will. Therefore, students need to pay close attention from the beginning and begin connecting the dots of what they learn as each day goes by.

And because I prove this fact to my students over and over ("Didn't I tell you we would see this again?" is my familiar refrain), they all quickly learn to take note (mentally and in writing) the first time. This type of purposeful iteration builds trust, ensures focus, and establishes familiarity and cohesion.

Purposeful, Quality Repetition

Unlike many English teachers, I'd never do something like an irony unit or a two-day lesson on irony and leave it at that. "Covering" a concept isn't effective teaching. In my class, if a student missed today's explanation and evidence of irony because of a trip to the nurse, there's no worry because every student will be exposed to this specific concept several more times this year.

If a student didn't get the concept of symbolism the first, second, or ninth time, you just bet when opportunity number ten comes around (and it will!), this will be the time when mastery occurs. Every student begins to feel comfortable and supported in a classroom like this; not just because the teacher creates a warm relationship and inviting class culture but because students have also been provided multiple chances to "get it" and to "get it" all.

Every student quickly feels a soothing sense of cohesion as they constantly traverse familiar territory, both conceptually and contextually. This will be a hallmark of your success as a facilitator, and if you've never taught in such a consistent and cohesive way, I encourage you to try it (Bruner, 2001).

All this consistency amongst a limited set of activities also makes planning much easier. With experience and based on content standards, an English teacher will have no problem in first determining the literary concepts and skills that are most important to focus upon. They'll also have tried out and tweaked many strategies for which to teach those concepts, so choosing the ones that work best is not a difficult decision.

In fact, the strategies teachers do chose work so well precisely because the teacher has practiced and expertly refined them year after year until these strategies are nothing short of superb. Suddenly, lesson planning becomes less overwhelming when a teacher has repertoire of literary concepts that can be plugged into another reliable repertoire of contexts (*how* students interact with and practice core concepts through a handful of great books).

None of this repetition gets boring because students are always being introduced to new books with which to interact. Plus, each fascinating book within itself is always changing, broadening, and deepening. The variety and complexity of a steady progression of new books brings English class to life and keeps routine contexts and activities written in the reader's notebooks fresh yet comfortingly familiar. Students end up retaining, mastering, and expanding upon this knowledge and these skills as they constantly are asked to go deeper and reach further. If a teacher can't do everything, then what they do must be done right, organically, and thoroughly.

Creating Context

This is not to say that you can't also *create* a context where your students practice a concept apart from waiting around for it to reoccur in a class novel. For example, if students only study similes when they occur naturally in a text, you can also devise other opportunities to reinforce this particular concept. You can have students identify similes in the independent books they're reading for homework, as well as in the independent novels on their desks. You can also have them act like the authors they've studied and create their own original similes in the narratives they compose.

Everything Old is New Again

As new literary content and information are introduced through the increasing number of novels we read together, I constantly have my students revisit and refer back to what came before. I ask them to connect the new books to the previous novels we've read so that meaning is reinforced. No longer do I simply "cover" something and go on, never to return; each succeeding novel has been strategically selected for the ways in which it's reflective of what came before in several significant ways.

And in terms of choosing a handful of novels that are reflective of each other, this won't be difficult because even the most seemingly unrelated novels are actually closely linked both in terms of literary conventions and themes. This thematic universality will be discussed further in Chapter 7.

The Disadvantages of Piecemeal Planning

You may know many teachers who plan unit by unit, even isolated lesson by isolated lesson, without a big picture and full slate of objectives in mind. The flaw with this piecemeal planning process is that it seriously impedes the laying of a strong footing and the erecting of adequate scaffolding that are required for all of your students to "get it" and to succeed.

How can teachers progressively build up their students towards comprehending challenging concepts and texts, as well as performing demanding skills, without clearly knowing far in advance what each progressive step will be? How will students feel both firmly grounded and adequately supported so that when those scaffolds are finally taken down, they can stand tall and achieve on their own—especially on testing day?

The other problem with such a shortsighted approach to planning is that some teachers too often come up short and thus shortchange their students as they always find themselves short on time. They either never seem to finish anything, they leave entire skills and concepts untouched, or they constantly scramble to add any old thing to fill up unintended extra time. They also jump from unit to unit in wild attempts to suddenly follow a pacing plan or meet a testing deadline.

Of course, the best of plans can go awry, run longer than expected, and be thwarted by interruptions, absences, and unscheduled changes; but facilitators always know exactly where they're headed, the best routes to take, and how much gas it will take to safely get their students to the final destination. They're also wise enough not to visit places they clearly don't have time for on this particular trip, no matter how tempting it may be to see it all. It is far better to teach with depth rather than breadth, and quality always trumps quantity.

Selecting a Small Repertoire of Literary Concepts

Of course, there are myriad ways of approaching, tackling, and understanding a literary concept, let alone for teaching English language arts itself, but it's recommended that you formulate a short list of the strategies you already know work best with your students. Using the recommendations in this book, as well as others you know, select a set of activities and graphic organizers that you've seen by experience are the most effective at providing your students with useful, transferable skills. This culling of the activities and assignments you *could use* into a small repertoire of techniques that your students *will consistently use* is important for several reasons.

First, you'll quickly discover that a small set of excellent activities your students interact with over and over gives them a greater chance of actually comprehending the concepts being taught. Sure, there's more than one way to skin a cat, but most of those ways work perfectly fine. Make a few informed choices and stick to the one or two approaches that successfully accomplish the same goal so your students can spend their time understanding, practicing, and applying, instead of wasting time learning yet another new approach. Don't confuse and distract your students with a never-ending series of convoluted or shiny new approaches to the same concept.

The reason why textbooks and curricular programs often offer a constant supply of new activities and graphic organizers for students to learn and use is because they want to keep things fresh. Yet this constant newness is ultimately counterproductive because the teacher spends too much time teaching students how to use this endless series of new approaches when the fact is that the first one or two worked just fine.

Focus on the few most effective, useful, and engaging activities, graphic organizers, and assignments. Using a whole-class novel approach, the stream of new chapter after exciting new chapter and new book after fabulous new book will provide plenty of novelty for students to enjoy without the teacher having to also reinvent the instructional wheel each time a literary concept is practiced.

For example, when you want your students to make an informed opinion about an important issue, always go to your Taking a Stand process. Your students already know what to do because they've participated in this activity a dozen times before. They get right down to business because the pro/con template is already waiting for them in their reader's notebooks. Plus, your students provide increasingly more intelligent responses because they've had so much practice with this effective process. Consistency and quality make all the difference, and my reader's notebooks provide the dependability students and teachers can count on for success.

Chapter 6.

Reading for Analysis and Inference

Every student—from developing to advanced to everything in between—benefits from curriculum, assignments, and activities that take them outside of themselves and their own little worlds. How can any person say they're only interested in a narrow range of topics, activities, or books if they haven't been consistently exposed to people, places, topics, situations, and novels that may be initially foreign, yet on closer examination, become astonishingly familiar?

As always, the answer is balance. There's ample room and reason for teachers and parents to honor a child's current individual interests and experiences, right along with exposing every child to the unknown, unexplored, and unexpected. This sense of mystery, wonder, and discovery about people and lands from long ago and far away leads to the openness and empathy that feed student wellbeing.

We owe such an expansive, experiential educational approach to our most needy students, just as much as to those who've already been officially labeled as gifted or talented. As educator and author Peg Grafwallner (2017) so wisely suggests, "…the next time you're tempted to refer to a student as 'struggling' or 'reluctant,' please consider eliminating that deficit thinking, and instead, replace with the word, 'developing.'"

When approached respectfully and strategically, all students rise to intellectual challenges, as well as to altruistic calls of duty. Similarly, every student feels prepared and validated to meet their teacher's high expectations when they've been given the proper support and encouragement to stretch their supposed, often self-imposed, limitations and illusions of separation from their fellow man.

The Four Bs of Effective, Expansive Instruction

The following four strategies will elevate and enrich any lesson so every student begins to see past boundaries, read between the lines, question the status quo, and uncover similarities.

1. **Beyond**

Intrepid teachers take each student beyond what they already know, believe, or think they're interested in. Teachers act as docents for glorious learning adventures and altruistic endeavors that challenge preconceptions and dissolve borders. Choosing great whole-class novels that draw in and captivate even initially skeptical students is a perfect way to accomplish this.

2. **Below the Surface**

Intuitive teachers also take students below the surface to discover new insights and connections that are often overlooked by the casual observer. As you teach your students to sift through the text (SIFT = symbols, irony, foreshadowing, and themes), they'll discover wonders that the majority of readers fail to ever notice.

3. **Back Inward**

Introspective teachers then take the group or the individual back inward to reflect upon their prior assumptions and to think critically about what they've learned, read, or experienced. Students' personal opinions, ideas, and interests can always be respected, but the personal can also be refined, enhanced, and amplified. Responding to a text is a crucial element of the reading process that will be explained in this chapter.

4. **Between**

Insightful teachers go one step further and provide their students with opportunities to make meaning between the growing number of texts they've read, lessons they've learned, and experiences they've engaged in. These potential connections allow every student to not only solidify their comprehension but to expand and comment upon that understanding. Patterns are exposed and parallels are drawn—the most important of which are the fundamental similarities that underlie all of nature and humanity.

Potential Pitfalls of Personalized Learning

Personalized learning tends to have two approaches: One is that each student's learning is tailored to their specific needs. The other is that students' personal interests drive the specifics of their own learning. The two are not mutually exclusive, but there are pitfalls to avoid with both.

In reference to the first approach, the more we circumscribe the scope of a student's learning by merely filling in gaps and shoring up weaknesses, the more we limit their overall growth and inhibit their joy of learning (National Education Policy Center, 2019). Re-teaching, remediation, acceleration, and computerized learning programs may have their place, but enrichment must be a staple of every student's learning. The Four Bs of Effective, Expansive Instruction above advocate for a learning experience that is equally comprehensive as it sometimes also must be customized.

In regard to the second approach, personalized learning shouldn't merely cater to students' narrow perspectives, practices, and proclivities because that can actually restrict their learning, even as students are ostensibly engaged and excited. Teaching does, at times, begin with the familiar and respects personal passions and meaning making; however, a teacher is always more concerned with *broadening* students' horizons and *expanding* their points of view and possibilities, rather than merely allowing them to chronically wallow in what is comfortable and customary.

Since growth and moving every child progressively forward are the goals, we never want students to be limited by their current personal interests, experiences, or abilities. Please think critically about the potential pitfalls of personalized learning so each student's interests are balanced with their full needs.

Teachers and parents can gently stretch the possibilities of each child and nudge kids past their preconceived notions of... *everything*—of what and who they like and are interested in, of what is important and what is trivial, and of what is regenerative and nourishing and what is toxic and empty.

There's room and reason in education for the currently comfortable, as well as the great unknown. Both have value, so allow each student to honor what they like, as well as to explore what just may become their new area of expertise or delight. My method of teaching major and minor whole-class novels right along with plenty of individual reading choice strikes a balance that will both please students and push them past their comfort zones.

Close Reading and Perceptive Writing

During the last two decades, you may have watched the wheels of curriculum and pedagogy turn. Standards have shifted, and Bloom's Taxonomy has blossomed. Such reevaluation of what is elemental and vital for students to be able to know and do is part of being a reflective and responsive educator.

That said, some core learning components should remain. Students must practice with, progress in, and perform six main skills:

1. Comprehending
2. Analyzing
3. Inferring
4. Explaining
5. Organizing
6. Responding

At least initially, these skills should be performed in this order because it is this same order that a person most often uses when attempting to understand and then write about a text or topic, and all of these skills will be explained in detail.

However, there are no hard and fast rules here. This process is just the most efficient way you can chunk and clarify the procedures for tackling difficult text and topics for your students. There doesn't need to be petty squabbling about whether this or that task is more analytical and less inferential or vice versa. The lines do blur, but the bottom line is that ultimately and increasingly your students can independently understand, speak about, and write about the texts they read in some significant, profound, and useful ways.

Eventually, some of your students will even begin to develop their own personal writing styles by creatively and confidently veering away from the foundational contexts you have taken such pains to provide for them. A true facilitator is pleased when their students are ready to shrug off their scaffolds and to stand tall on their own! In fact, such independence is what a facilitator is always working toward.

Why We Read

Mainly, people read for pleasure, perspective, passion, and even provocation. The sheer thrill, practical insight, awe-inspiring wonder, golden wisdom, and raw emotion that are present in any text must always be featured in a fascinating classroom, whether you're reading literary narrative fiction or any type of non-fiction. Please don't make the horrible mistake of overlooking, trivializing, or downplaying any of the captivating excitement, humor, drama, suspense, passion, or natural curiosity that a text may engender! Tacking difficult text should never be a cold or clinical endeavor.

Comprehending

Of course, students must read first to understand the information, argument, or story being presented in a text because without that basic and fundamental comprehension, they will neither enjoy nor learn from the text before them. Give your students the image of a magnifying glass to emphasize that we must see the text clearly.

Understanding includes the basic plot or situations, characters or people, and settings (times, dates, and places) in narrative texts, both in fiction and non-fiction or historical texts. My reader's notebooks purposely begin with key vocabulary, settings, and characters to assist with the basic comprehension so crucial for deeper discussions and writing prompts related to a text.

Comprehension also includes determining the topic and main idea in informational texts, as well as the major examples and significant details that support that main idea. In argumentative texts, the students must determine the topic and author's claim, as well as the author's major points and evidence. Depending on the complexity of the text, full comprehension can be a daunting task for even the most advanced students.

Types of Comprehension Questions

To assist in your students' comprehension, class discussions, notes, and questions can include the content of the text. These are the "right there" facts or the "when, where, who, and what?" of the reading that students must find directly in the text. Constantly refer to and ask about these essential components of the text, even as you go deeper into analysis and interpretation, because if you ever neglect the fundamental nuts and bolts of a text, many students will lose their way.

Just because the teacher may have read the text at hand dozens of times, they must constantly supplement their students' foundational understanding of the text (which students probably have only read once) so that students are always on solid ground. Only then can a student start digging deeper and discover gold. The reason why kids often cannot read between the lines and go deeper is because they've only ever been on shaky ground with a text. Then when they're asked to dig deeper, the ground quickly gives way and caves in on itself—and on them!

The Necessity of Notes

With narrative texts, students should have a list of important characters or historical figures (each with an appositive that tells something to easily identify who that specific person is) and a list of major settings (times and places). To reinforce the necessity of these lists, require your students to turn to their notes when during discussions they say things like, "I forget his name but…" or use a pronoun with no antecedent. Do not feed the student the character's forgotten name and do not allow other students to call out the answer in an effort to "help." This requirement of using one's notes as an essential tool proves to students that true note taking is indispensable.

Creating Contextual Clues

Likewise, each time you turn to a page in the text where you'll be asking questions that require the skills of analysis or inference, begin with a very quick comprehension review. Call on students to first remind you "where" we are on this page (the setting) and "who" is there (the names of the characters present). This immediately creates a context for every student, from developing to advanced, to begin to remember what went on that page so that when you delve deeper into the text they'll have the best chance possible of succeeding.

Training students not to reread every single word but to strategically scan through a page of the text they've previously read in order to reestablish the context at hand is a skill your students must practice constantly to increase both their speed and accuracy of answering "right there" questions. So many of our students simply stare at a page of text as though they're expecting the answer to spontaneously jump out at them. Students need to be trained to engage with text, and always referring back to the basics helps them gain a foothold from which to progress.

Comprehending Informational and Argumentative Texts

This constant but quick contextualizing of everything that you will have the students go on to analyze and interpret can be transferred to informational and argumentative texts as well. Students can have notes in the form of an outline of what they comprehended from these types of texts. They can also have a graphic organizer of the author's main idea or argument and the major examples and evidence the author used to support their thesis.

When you want your students to analyze or make inferences about a certain passage, first ask them to remind you of the main idea and which particular point the author is discussing in that passage. This brief time you spend checking for and reinforcing comprehension will serve your students well.

It will also immediately alert you to those times when all their prior comprehension actually went in one ear and out the other because right now your students cannot seem to answer any of your most basic questions! As demoralizing as this is, a teacher must know when this disconnect is occurring (and with what frequency with certain students) because it clearly shows you that your students are nowhere near ready to go deeper into this text.

Deep Understanding Leads to Deeper Appreciation

Of course, there's so much more than mere understanding awaiting your students when they have a facilitator to guide them through a text, especially a long and/or difficult piece. Always remind your students that besides reading for pleasure and basic understanding, in your class they're also *studying* the text—and on a very deep level at that.

It's always a mixed blessing when you must answer "No" to your students' eager queries of "Are we reading today?!" On one hand, you love their excitement for and engagement with your fascinating novel. On the other hand, you have to reinforce the fact that we cannot possibly read further until they have thoroughly explored all that this text has to offer thus far; not because we're too busy right now going over useless, isolated, pedantic English exercises vaguely related to the text, but because the depth in which students understand this rich text now will pay off for them later.

In fact, there's no way they could fully appreciate what will be coming next in this profound and powerful novel unless students fully comprehend what we've read thus far. And if you've crafted your instruction with equal parts soulful and academic learning, your students will enjoy the challenges that analysis and inference have to offer *just as much* as reading the next exciting chapter or interesting article!

Analyzing

When you're about to move on to analysis, give your students the image of an x-ray to point out that they must now look below the surface to discover "the bones" of the text and how it's all held together. Exposing the underlying structure of a text allows students to understand *how* the author lets the story unravel, presents their information, or supports their claims. This examination of the *construct* of the text reveals the author's means and methods in putting together this text. This analysis also shows how the parts relate to each other and come together to make a worthwhile and cohesive whole.

Use academic vocabulary when analyzing the text's components. Discuss the author's style to ascertain and appreciate the techniques they used. This taking apart or deconstructing of the text reveals both the writer's purpose and their careful organization. This type of analysis also models for your students what the components of good writing look like so students can begin to develop a style of their own. Until they do develop that personal writing style, your students will be able to write *like* certain authors and use their underlying structures onto which students can hang their own words and ideas.

Types of Analysis Questions

In general, with analysis you're continuing to ask "right there" questions that can be found directly in the text and therefore be supported by textual evidence or source citations. Often, however, analysis also asks "taking it apart" or "pulling it together" questions that may begin with *how* and *which*. Questions that ask students to identify patterns and trends within the text require more complex answers that often may be found by referring to different parts of the text. Again, academic vocabulary is a feature of analysis and may be used in these types of questions.

Analyzing Narrative Texts

With narrative texts, techniques like chronology and the use of flashbacks are discussed, as well as how the chapters are constructed. Students can also identify the narrator and point of view. The author's use of dialogue, humor, suspense, and surprise are discussed and how all these choices shape the reader's experience. Suddenly, your students see the author's artistry and craft as we reveal the meanings behind their use of figurative language. The specifics of whichever genre students are reading are explicitly noted as well.

The Problem with Plot Charts

One common analysis technique for narrative text that I avoid is any kind of plot chart. I've found it completely fruitless and frustrating to try to pigeonhole a wonderfully crafted novel into distinct components, such as exposition, rising action, climax, falling action, and resolution.

Instead, I find that simply discussing who the protagonists and antagonists are, as well as what constitutes all the potential conflicts between them, is enough in terms of defining the central plot structure of the story.

Analyzing Informational and Argumentative Texts

Many informational and argumentative texts look very little like the typical five-paragraph essays we take such pains to get our students to master, so a careful picking apart of these texts serves our students well and augments their comprehension.

How the text is framed by an introduction and a conclusion can be examined, and the components of each can be articulated. Effective introductions and conclusions are some of the most difficult things for students to write, so look for the writer's craft in hooking their audience and how the author wraps up at the ending of their piece. (This will be discussed further in Chapter 11.)

Teachers demand clear thesis statements, but often it's difficult to find *the* thesis in a complex text. How does the author let us know the broad topic of the text, and how do they narrow it down to a main idea about or opinion of that topic?

Your students already have comprehended the author's major examples and evidence, but how does the author make these separate ideas flow together? Students can identify the use of transitions and their varied effects. Also, look for examples of complex and compound sentences and discuss the author's use of titles, headings, graphs, charts, and tables, and their intended audience.

Inferring

Next, move from the explicit, denotative, and literal level of comprehension and analysis toward an even deeper reading of the text. Give your students the image of brain scan to show that it's now time to get into the author's mind. Show them a picture of an x-ray in black and white and an MRI full of neon colors illuminating a person's brain in order to show the contrast between analysis and inference.

Your students are beginning to see that there's more than meets the eye, and it may take more than one reading of the text to figure everything out, especially in terms what the author was thinking or intended. Students will have to dig deeper to deduce what else the text holds for the reader, including the inner thoughts, feelings, and motivations of the characters or historical figures.

Now students have to think even more carefully about the text to make sense of the implicit information and themes of the text. They move beyond mere information and basic structure to focus upon the author's message and why the author wrote what they did. Students read between the lines by surmising, hypothesizing, and coming to conclusions to see the author's subtext and connotative meanings.

Types of Inference Questions

In terms of inference, generally you'll be formulating questions that ask *why*. These answers will be based not entirely on the text, as with comprehension and analysis questions, but now will be based on an interaction between "the text and me." Therefore, an explanation will be required in order to clarify what specific part/s of the text led your students to their answers.

Making Inferences about Narrative Texts

With narrative texts, students move beyond plot to identifying the underlying themes or important life lessons and wisdom the author wants to convey through story. Using inference, students focus on meaning and motivation, both the author's and the characters' motivations. Literary devices like irony, foreshadowing, and symbols show students that a narrative story has subtle humor, intricate planning, and hidden messages the author is hoping the reader can identify and interpret.

Making Inferences about Informational and Argumentative Texts

In informational and argumentative texts, students can infer the possible implications of the facts being presented. They also surmise any ulterior motives, biases, or unspoken agendas the author may harbor. Students explore the author's tone and personal perspective. They do not move into the realm of critique or evaluation just yet, however. At this juncture, students should be more concerned with revealing the author's sense of passion or import for their subject, rather than each student's personal opinions.

The Validating Properties of Inference

Most of all, students learn through inference that the author is expecting the reader to be a partner in the reading process. The author doesn't need to spell out everything for us, nor should we expect them to. The author rightly assumes we will use our background knowledge, experiences, and intuition in order to fill in the blanks of the text. The author expects us to be an active, rather than passive, reader.

Making inferences should be fun and fascinating because students move from investigating to finding solutions for the secret meanings in the text. From magnifying glass to x-ray to MRI, your student sleuths eventually crack the case every time! They move from the content and construct of the text to the *context* in which the author intended it. All of their scrutinizing becomes well worth the effort because students discover that the text is full, rich, and deep. It has an abundance of useful insight, wisdom, important ideas, and implications from which the careful reader can benefit.

A facilitator also wants their students to apprehend that the author of a narrative has absolute respect for their reader. Even young adult novels can be extremely profound, complex, and subtle, and you must stress to your students that the author has every faith that the reader is fully capable of appreciating and benefiting from all the wit and depth that this text has to offer, even if it may take some heavy thinking!

Tell your students, "The author wrote this book precisely for students like you at your age. Therefore, we must all accept the author's invitation into intellect and wisdom and rise to the occasion!"

Even with informational and argumentative texts, which were likely written for an adult audience, the author not only wants their audience to be active readers but informed and thoughtful readers who can do some of the heavy lifting for themselves. In fact, most authors were probably writing under a word or page count constraint and desperately expect their readers to fill in some of the blanks for themselves.

All of this is vital for students to understand because without being readers who apply themselves to the full understanding and grandeur of the text, our students remain only functionally literate. The delicate balance between the necessary holding of our students' hands and the goal of allowing them to walk on their own is something a facilitator always has to be aware of. We never want to create an environment of dependency and passivity for our students, who usually are more than willing to let the teacher do all the work for them.

Explaining

Making inferences is surmising and coming to conclusions about what one *thinks* the author means. One could be wrong, however, and different students may make different inferences. Students can only rely on their logical understanding of the examples and evidence they found during their comprehension and analysis.

This is why explanation and interpretation are key to making inferences. It's always incumbent upon the students to explain how and why they reached their conclusions based on what the text says (hence, the "text" component in a "text and me" question). Students must justify and elaborate on their assumptions.

Therefore, for explanation you now can give your students the image of a sparkling diamond to show them that they must explain their reasoning and make their inferences crystal clear. Your students have moved from investigating to surmising to *proving* their theories with a combination of facts from the text and their own ideas. This is another fascinating opportunity for your students to reveal their own personal reasoning and reckoning as to what they believe the author intended or what insights the reader should gain.

Organizing

After such a thorough understanding of the text using both denotative and connotative reasoning (as well as literal and figurative reasoning and explicit and implicit reasoning), you can now have your students objectively delineate, describe, define, trace, outline, or summarize the text in their own words. Depending on what level of analysis is required, students can also cite passages from the text as examples, evidence, facts, or data to back up their ideas.

No matter what authentic assessment you may choose to give your students in order to gauge their analysis of the text—be it an oral, written, or multimedia presentation—they must do some planning and organizing first in order to perform this reconstruction of the text. All the important information that their analysis and inferences yielded must be synthesized and ordered. Students must take what they found to be essential and vital in the text and give all those pieces clear form, structure, and cohesion. They must identify patterns in the text so that seemingly disparate pieces of information and meaning can be condensed and grouped.

Initially, guide your students through and give them copious practice with the major components of an essay: title, introduction, thesis statement, examples, evidence, citations (textual evidence), explanation, inference, response, and conclusion.

Also, provide students with graphic organizers, such as essay webs with different shapes that correspond to the different parts of the essay to help your students when they must give order to a major writing assignment. You may give students the image of a roadmap to show them that even though there may be many routes to arrive at a destination, one must choose the clearest direction and stick with their plan.

Of course, also focus on cohesion and the use of appropriate transitions. Once students have a thorough understanding of what a basic essay should look like, it's always an ongoing process for your students to both analyze increasingly longer and more demanding texts and to then organize that information framed by their own words.

Responding

There's one more step beyond comprehending, analyzing, inferring, explaining, and organizing that your students must master. Without response, what students have done thus far is mostly reporting or research—albeit in-depth and thorough reporting and research at that.

There are many occasions when "just the facts, ma'am" will suffice and one's personal ideas and opinions are not asked for, appropriate, or appreciated. Yet that kind of writing leaves your students and their personal ideas completely out of the picture.

Sure, inferring required supposition on the students' part but only in so far as getting into the mind of the author or the motivation of the character. Now it's your students' chance to independently speak their *own* minds in response to the text. The roles are now reversed, and the learning becomes much more active as your students step in as the expert and they stand toe to toe with the author.

A part of this whole process of interacting with text must feature each individual student because injecting personal interpretations and opinions into an otherwise factual account is the hallmark of true essay writing and is also a critical component in making your instruction truly fascinating. The difference between an essay and a report is that the writer of the essay is *expected* to convey their personal point of view about the subject and its content. Investment and engagement are naturally built into responding, reacting, critical thinking, and editorializing (*Edutopia*, 2016).

Now give your students the image of a spotlight to convey that responding is about them individually shedding new light and fresh ideas on the text. They are now to make *their own* meaning of what they found in the text. Students are to draw their own conclusions about the information they discovered. After clearly writing about their understanding of what the author was trying to convey in the text, now students come in as an external authority.

This is such an important final step in giving your students voice, choice, and confidence in their own ideas, knowledge, opinions, and experiences. If you expect your students to act like scholars and intellectuals, then allow them the frequent opportunity to express their own insights, beliefs, judgments, and connections *as they relate to the text*. Student response should be a cornerstone of your ELA class because it values and develops creativity and critical thinking, and it is from these places that interest, innovation, and invention spring.

Responding is a "mostly me" endeavor that begins in the text and then is taken beyond the page by the individual student. As a guide, you can give your students four avenues of response to explore: countering/contrasting, commenting, connecting/comparing, and critiquing. (These are further explored in Chapter 11.) Another fascinating motivator is that students are free to choose one or many avenues when responding to a text—both when responding to the text in its entirety or when focusing on specific aspects of the text.

One reason why students don't write well is because they have nothing to write about beyond their own experiences and opinions—and those may be limited and uninformed. Since you place *equal* value in personal responses as well as objective reporting, training your students to deeply understand and to explain their perceptive insights into texts that initially appear far removed from their world becomes doubly important: Students need the skills of comprehension, analysis, inference, explanation, and organization not only to prove they have a thorough understanding of the text but also so they can transform that which began as foreign into something inextricably familiar and personally indispensable.

Chapter 7.

Whole-Class Literature Discussions

As a true facilitator, never drop your students into the wilderness of rigorous standards and difficult text unprepared and allow them to fend for themselves. Oh, you love to challenge them and let students wrestle with the hard stuff, and they love it too—*if* you've supported them along the way. Have effective structures in place so when you ask your students to comprehend and construct they have the necessary tools to do so.

The Difference Between a Teacher and a Facilitator

A facilitator's main goal is to move their students forward toward greater independence. A facilitator's students don't need their teacher any less, however. It's just that the facilitator has found the most effective and efficient ways to transfer knowledge and skills so that almost immediately and with increasing levels of complexity, their students are able to *apply* that knowledge and those skills in worthwhile and profound ways. A facilitator asks their students to regurgitate information far less than they ask them to analyze, make inferences about, explain, organize, and respond to that information.

Two Teaching Approaches

A teacher has two basic choices: On one hand, they can spend the majority of their time *telling* their students what they should know. A teacher can simply point out to their students the things that the teacher deems important. This manner of direct instruction and lecturing is admittedly easier and faster than facilitating learning. It's also very validating for the teacher who's the expert imparting wisdom to their students: *Wow, look how smart this teacher is!* No student gets the chance to find or figure out what's important on their own because the teacher is too busy "teaching," covering the curriculum, and merely exposing their students to the standards.

This is how I taught initially. My students were dependent on my expertise, and this is how I thought it should be because this is how I was taught in the 1970s.

On the other hand, a teacher can point their students in the right direction by strategically providing them with increasingly complex and rich text and curriculum and then posing carefully crafted questions that *allow the students themselves* to tell the teacher what they found and understood. Students are given the coaching, the chance, the challenge, the confidence, and ultimately, the glory.

I'm thrilled to hand over the power and the prestige to my well prepared and eager students. Facilitation stresses active learning over passive instructing. Facilitation works hand in hand with fascination and fairness so the students feel at the *center of the action*. Now instead of always being didactic, I allow my students to discover for themselves. Discovery lets the *students* feel like the smart ones in the class.

I always give my students first crack at things, even things I may initially assume are beyond their current reach. I regularly shut up, step back, and see what they come up with. I have guided them, modeled, or held their hand just enough; now I want to see if they have the chops and the confidence to handle the tough stuff on their own. I become their resource and sounding board. I simply make managing their own learning possible and practical because I've provided structured opportunities and experiences that grease the wheels of my students' minds.

It's not that I've abandoned my students, that they do not need me, or that I've suddenly made myself superfluous. On the contrary, I'm always there as their guide and guru: to push and encourage, to nudge and finesse, to fill in any blanks they have left, to point out what they've overlooked, to clear up any misconceptions they may have, and then to take them to the next level ever more deeply or more quickly. I'm also there to be open to and celebrate their insights that vary from mine or that had completely escaped my notice.

Oh, my students still need me plenty—but in different (and much better) ways than before.

Fake Facilitation

Conversely, I observe too many classrooms where the students are constantly working in groups yet are merely working cooperatively on tasks they could readily accomplish individually. Rarely do I see true collaboration and a true necessity for interaction, let alone teamwork. There's a lot of chatter, but I hear precious few substantive conversations. The atmosphere is more casual and less serious, as if nothing of great import or meaning is being undertaken. (Read more about true collaboration in Chapter 9.)

Even worse, I see the students working on assignment after assignment they not only can do by themselves but for which they really didn't need their teacher at all. Oh, the teacher was there to assign and explain the particular tasks, but the students weren't being pushed past their current levels of proficiency. Except in the most superficial ways, these teachers made themselves unnecessary.

I would argue, however, that everyone at every level can benefit from an excellent educator. See, I believe in education. I believe in the enduring value of having a living, breathing expert standing before and interacting with a classroom full of students—who are also living, breathing youngsters who need structure, support, stimulation, and sound guidance. Not a screen, not a monitor, not a projection, not a hologram, not a computer program, not a website, but a firm, fair, fascinating, flesh-and-blood facilitator like you (Ellsworth, 2001).

Unfortunately, fake facilitating seems to be becoming the norm, even in many college classes. The professor throws the students into groups, presents the current assignment (usually based on some book or article), and then steps away to allow the students to do all the work—work and reading they probably could've done on their own before they had ever stepped foot in this class! Besides the fact that the professor need only supervise (and superficially at that) and answer questions here and there (mostly about how this group project will be graded), the teacher then gets the added luxury of simply sitting back and watching only a handful of group presentations a few times per semester and then doling out the same grade to each member of each group!

I personally get nothing out of educational situations like this. If I'm going to pay handsomely for a class, I want to benefit directly from the expertise of my professor. I'm quite proficient at working on my own or collaborating with colleagues without having to pay for any of it. I want to be enlightened, broadened, pushed, provoked, challenged, coached, and mentored by an acknowledged expert, preferably someone who is always at least a few levels above me in wisdom, proficiency, and experience. And I believe all of our students want much of the same thing and deserve nothing less. A teacher should be interactive, indispensable, and deeply interested in their students.

Moving from teaching to true facilitating comes, of course, with its own learning curve. Expect that the same lesson, article, or book you used to teach will take much longer when properly facilitated. The way you craft, sequence, and group your questions may forever be a painstaking part of your lesson planning as you constantly refine, add to, and delete certain parts that no longer satisfy you. Rigor is a two-way street, but this extra time scrutinizing and structuring your lessons and activities will reap great rewards.

You must also be willing to relinquish your seat in your ivory tower, to get off your butt, and to mingle with the masses. Faster, easier, and self-aggrandizing facilitating is not. Actually seeing your students grow before your eyes, think and try hard, not be allowed give up, truly collaborate as well as cooperate, go deeper into a concept or text than they've ever gone before, and achieve success are the rewards of choosing facilitation over teaching.

Literary Themes

The last literary device documented in the reader's notebook is literary themes. Under the heading, *Theme Category Examples,* my students write this definition of a theme on the left-hand side of their reader's notebooks:

A theme is the message or moral of the story. A theme is also the wisdom, life lesson, or useful advice the author taught the reader.

I explain to my students that a great author wants to do two things at the same time: Authors want to *tell* you an exciting, interesting, moving story, but they also want to *teach* you important lessons that can improve your life.

On the left-hand pages of the theme sections of their reader's notebooks, students list the themes as we identify them in the novels we're reading. We also put a +, -, or ~ symbol in front of each theme category to generally denote their positive, negative, or multifaceted natures. On the right-hand pages, students write the page number evidence for each time a theme is identified in the novel.

Theme Category Examples

For your reference, here is a master list of the theme categories that most often reoccur in young adult novels, listed in no particular order. Keep in mind that these are broad categories of literary themes, not themes in themselves.

For example, *lying* is a broad theme category, while "*Lying can cause others to distrust not only what you have recently said and will say but all of what you have said before"* is a theme that coveys a specific lesson from the book *Shiloh* and gives the reader specific insight about the consequences of telling lies.

- Lying and hiding the truth
- Telling the truth
- Good and bad reputations
- Physical abuse and neglect
- Hiding or holding in feelings
- Expressing feelings
- Poverty
- Shame and embarrassment
- Betrayal
- Prejudice and discrimination
- Breaking negative stereotypes
- Reinforcing negative stereotypes
- Rejecting difference
- Resisting change
- Putting others first and sacrifice
- Putting yourself first
- Foolish pride
- Swallowing your pride
- Ignoring hateful people
- Going along with the crowd
- Going against the crowd
- Picking your battles: standing up for yourself
- Picking your battles: backing down
- Appreciating what you have
- Trusting
- Not trusting
- Caring
- Not caring
- Self-respect and dignity
- Compromising yourself
- Changing yourself for the better
- Being humane
- Being non-confrontational
- Protecting others
- The value of friendship and belonging
- Loyalty
- Supporting others
- Bitterness
- Being sensitive
- Revenge
- Misplaced revenge
- Paying consequences
- Unintended consequences
- Guilt and regret
- Good and bad influences
- Focusing on the positive
- Taking responsibility for what you did wrong
- Hope
- Hopelessness, suicide
- Blaming others, not taking responsibility
- Holding a grudge
- Apologizing
- Forgiveness
- Sympathy and empathy
- Bravery and courage
- Minding your own business
- Getting involved
- Giving up
- Perseverance
- Judging others
- Tough love
- Teaching kids a lesson
- Allowing a kid to act like an adult
- Being a bystander
- Rescuing or saving others

I can say with confidence and from personal life experience that this list of theme categories allows children to explore most of the major issues they will face in their lifetimes and that the majority of books that explore these themes provide wise guidance for how to make positive life choices. If this isn't reaching the whole child, I don't know what is.

Class Discussion Prompts for Narrative Texts

The following are the most frequent ways I craft the questions I put forth to my students when we're discussing a whole-class novel. Note that these "questions" are stated in the form of an answer prompt that asks the students to do some form of comprehending, analyzing, inferring, explaining, or responding that was explained in the previous chapter. As Truby (2019) suggests, "Ask questions that draw from the text and require evidence to support theme."

Evidence

- Provide evidence that proves
- Provide ___ pieces of evidence that prove
- Provide ___ reasons why

Clarification (explaining why and how)

- Make an inference about
- Read between the lines and explain
- Explain why
- Explain the *real reason* why
- Explain what _____ *really* did when
- Explain what _____ did to/for _____
- Explain what _____ was willing to do when
- Explain what _____ was trying to do when
- Explain what _____ expected would happen and then what *actually* happened when
- Explain _____'s motivation for choosing to/not to
- Explain _____'s reasons for
- Explain why _____ choosing to _____ would be a bad/good idea.
- Explain what _____ realized when
- Explain _____'s opinion of
- Analyze/explain how
- Explain how _____ was able to
- Explain how _____ reacted when

- Describe _____'s reaction to
- Explain how _____ responded to
- Explain the significance/importance of
- Explain the meaning of

Compare and contrast

- Compare and contrast _____ and _____.
- Explain how _____ and _____ are similar.
- Explain which other character is most like_____.
- Explain the differences between _____ and _____.
- Make a connection to
- Connect _____ to something we have seen before.
- Connect how
- Explain how _____'s advice is similar to
- Explain who also

Change

- Explain how _____ has changed.
- Explain how _____ has changed since
- Explain what _____ did for the first time.
- Explain what _____ finally did that s/he could not do before.

Wisdom

- Explain what lesson _____ has learned.
- Explain what _____'s advice was to _____.
- Explain why _____ advised _____ to
- Explain the lesson that _____ taught to _____.
- Explain how _____ solved the problem of
- Explain what strategy/wisdom _____ used when

Character Relationships

- Explain how _____ was a good friend to/supportive of _____.
- Explain how _____ was a bad friend to/unsupportive of _____.
- Explain what _____ blamed _____ for.
- Explain why _____ holds a grudge against _____.

- Explain how _____ treated _____.
- Explain what _____ and _____ disagree about.
- Explain how _____ got _____ to
- Explain who won the argument between
- Explain who lost the battle between
- Explain why _____ forgave _____.

Motivation

- Describe how _____ felt when
- Explain what _____ wanted when
- Explain what _____ most wants/desires/longs for.
- Explain what _____ was afraid of when
- Explain what _____ is most afraid of.
- Explain why _____ has difficulty handling/dealing/coping with

Choices and consequences

- Explain the risk of
- Explain what _____ is risking when
- Explain what the worst thing is about
- Explain the danger of
- Explain what is tragic about
- Explain what _____ won/gained by
- Explain what _____ lost when/by
- Explain what _____ decided when
- Explain what decision _____ made when
- Explain the consequence of
- Explain the unintended consequence of
- Explain what _____ is willing to do now that
- Explain what _____ is willing/ready to do if
- Explain why _____ was heroic when
- Explain what consequences _____ paid for
- Explain how _____ could have prevented

Commentary, Evaluation, Judgment

- Take a stand on
- Justify why
- Suppose that
- Even if
- Explain why you think it was right to
- Explain what you think _____ should
- Explain why _____ should or should not have
- Explain why _____ made a good or bad choice when
- Explain why you agree or disagree with _____ when
- Explain who was at fault when
- Explain who was to blame for
- Explain who was responsible for

Irony

- Explain what is ironic about

Symbols

- Identify and interpret the symbol on page

Vocabulary

- Use a vocabulary word to describe

Predictions and Foreshadowing

- Predict what will happen now that
- Predict _____'s reaction to
- Predict what might have happened if
- Explain what you should have predicted
- Explain how _____ was foreshadowed
- Explain how we should have known that _____ would happen.
- Besides _____, explain who else you think will

Alternatives

- Explain what _____ could have done instead of

Going deeper

- Ostensibly,
- On the surface,
- At first glance,
- One would think

Themes

- Provide the theme category that describes _____ when
- Provide ___ theme categories you can identify in the scene where

Class Discussion Examples

Here are some representative class discussion prompts from the following books and films. Whether or not you've read these books, seen these movies, or remember these details, you can begin to see the type of depth, analysis, and inference that I require from my students.

From *Shiloh*:

- This is a "right there" question. From chapter 1 and 2, provide seven different pieces of evidence that Marty is humane.
- Explain the underlying reason why Judd abuses his dogs.
- Explain who won the argument between Marty and Dad in chapter 10.

From *The Watsons Go to Birmingham—1963*:

- Use 10 vocabulary words to explain why Kenny and Byron have to scrape the ice off of the Brown Bomber's windows.
- Explain what two theme categories helped Rufus and Kenny become friends again.
- Compare and contrast Byron and Kenny's reactions to the dead dove and explain why they each felt so differently.
- Explain the *real* reason why Momma and Dad are sending By to Birmingham.

From *Seabiscuit*:

- Explain how the director foreshadowed Red's blindness in one eye.

- After his tragic injury, describe Red when he tells Charles Howard, "Don't scratch. Call Wolfe."

- Explain why, out of all the other characters, Charles Howard is the most afraid of Red being killed if he races again.

From *There's a Boy in the Girls' Bathroom*:

- Explain the mistakes both Mrs. Chalkers and Jeff made with Bradley in chapter 5.

- In chapter 13 and 14, provide three pieces of evidence that prove Bradley is beginning to change for the better.

- Explain what Bradley was expecting from Jeff and what Jeff actually did when Bradley was alone in the far corner of the playground.

- In chapter 17, provide three theme categories that describe Jeff when he met Robbie and the boys.

- In chapter 27, provide nine different pieces of evidence of Bradley's positive choices while in Carla's office.

- Create a brand new theme category that explains why everybody likes and trusts Bradley now.

- Turn to your list of characters. Besides Carla, explain who you would nominate as the most supportive character in the book.

From *Roll of Thunder, Hear My Cry*:

- In chapter 3, explain how Big Ma's advice to Little Man is similar to another character's philosophy.

- Explain the real reason why Mr. Morrison was mad that Stacey fought T.J. at the Wallace Store.

- Explain what Uncle Hammer could have done to help Cassie, instead of rushing out of the house to get revenge on Mr. Simms.

- After Papa ignores Mr. Jamison's warnings not to move forward with the boycott, explain what is ironic about Papa's decision.

- Provide nine different pieces of evidence that prove Cassie got smart and safe revenge on Lillian Jean.

- Make an inference and explain the probable unintended consequences of Cassie's revenge on Lillian Jean.

From *Guess Who's Coming to Dinner?*:

- What plot device does the screenwriter use to heighten the drama and emotions of the movie?
- Explain why Monsignor Mike Ryan says that interracial marriages sometimes work out better.
- Identify and interpret the symbol in the scene between Matt and Christina at the drive-in diner.

From *The Outsiders*:

- Compare and contrast these three sets of parents: Darry as Ponyboy's guardian, Mr. and Mrs. Cade as Johnny's parents, and Mr. and Mrs. Sheldon as Bob's parents.
- Make an inference and explain why Ponyboy chooses to tell Darry about having his recurring nightmare last night, when Pony knows this will only make Darry more worried than he already is.
- Explain the real reason why Sandy's parents sent her to Florida to live with her grandparents.
- Explain the real reason why Cherry refuses to see Johnny in the hospital.
- Explain the meaning of Ponyboy speaking to us in parenthesis for the first time in chapter 9.

These discussion questions challenge students to dig deeply and to consider all angles. With modeling, practice, and encouragement, even the most hesitant student with developing skills will eventually rise to the occasion and triumph!

Paying Attention

As I wrote in *The Firm, Fair, Fascinating Facilitator* (Ward, 2015), a potent way to make your students feel important, recognized, and validated is to refer back to their comments, answers, questions, and ideas during class discussions. Referencing what a student has previously said and giving them full credit for having said it engenders positive feelings that are significant, lasting, and infectious.

Suddenly everyone wants their voice heard in the hope that it'll be important and useful enough to be referred to later—whether that reference is moments from now, a few days from now, or not until next semester. Without being patronizing or phony about it, recall aloud the comments specific students have so thoughtfully and confidently shared in the past any time you see a legitimate and useful connection to what's currently being discussed or presented.

Such acknowledgement can take many forms:

- "And now with this additional example, we can see why Nina was so correct a moment ago."
- "As Shane brought up last week…"
- "So, now let's build on the ideas that Kim and Kenny were just talking about."
- "José, this is similar to your comment about…"
- "Vivian, remember when I told you weeks ago that we would see again what you had pointed out about…"

Yes, your advanced students will be delighted as always to be recognized, but your developing students had barely come down from the high of saying something intelligent the first time. Imagine their pride as they find out that double-dipping isn't only allowed in your class but that you dish out the second scoop yourself!

This personalizing takes but a moment of time yet has a tremendous impact on your students. Use it liberally and with gusto. This is a skill that comes very easily to teachers who genuinely enjoy listening to what their students have to say and therefore remember their students' comments well. You can amaze your students when you reference something they had said days before, even when they themselves don't immediately recall having said it.

Sincerely Care about What Your Students Have to Say

If all this remembering seems like it would be difficult for you, just *listen more attentively* to what your students say. If what they have to say is honestly not very interesting or significant to you, then *you* are doing something wrong. You're not asking the right questions, and/or you're not giving your students the background knowledge and skills to speak with intelligence. Perhaps you're not providing the inspiration for your students to speak from the heart.

Every teacher can cultivate this wonderfully validating tool of a keen memory to prove to their students that their participation and ideas count in very useful and important ways. Even if you don't quite remember exactly who said what every time, it's perfectly okay to ask the class something like, "Who did I say I needed to hear more from?" or "I'm sorry, who just said…?" The fact that your students can sometimes remember for you demonstrates that they're keenly listening as well!

Glorious Gold Stars

My offering of what I call Gold Star questions is something that has worked exceedingly well for me in regards to motivating my students to push themselves to think deeply. Some of the most profound aspects of my curriculum that I once assumed were beyond the current scope of my students' abilities have now become fodder for me to challenge them to go further than where they've previously gone.

Challenge is a great motivator. I guarantee you that with the right combination of the encouragement that teacher fairness creates and the fundamental capabilities and knowledge that facilitation provides, your students will not only enthusiastically rise to your fascinating challenges, they'll often meet them with confidence and success.

It no longer matters to me if I initially think that some particular insight, analysis, or interpretation is beyond my students' current grasp. I'm going to offer up this opportunity for depth by challenging all of my students in all of my classes when two essential criteria are met.

One: When this information is vital to a thorough and deep understanding of the text or topic at hand, then I cannot in good conscience overlook it. I won't underestimate or shortchange any of my students, regardless of any labels that have been placed upon them. I will instead respect every student's potential, inspire their determination, and provide the supports they need along the way to rise to the occasion.

Two: When this vital knowledge or insight is actually there, then it must be addressed. Either the author intentionally placed it there and wants it to be noticed; or else it's there naturally, and this happy accident is worth paying attention to. This doesn't mean that every nuance needs to be pointed out and picked apart; but it does mean that I neither gloss over what an author intended us to note or to ponder, nor will I ignore some inherently important fact, revelation, or connection in regards to the book we're studying—no matter how over my students' heads it seems.

No set of standards can ever direct you towards every place worthy of taking your students. As a perceptive teacher, focus on that which you know to be interesting, relevant, and rich. Then craft your instruction and develop questions that will allow your students to discover these insights for themselves.

Often, my most challenging and profound Gold Star questions are asking for patterns or contrasts that may not be readily apparent but are there nonetheless. As I link what the class has previously discussed to what we're presently discussing, I regularly tell my students, "You all know this answer. You may not *know* you know the answer, but I guarantee that you do. So, take a moment now to figure this one out for yourselves because it's completely within your grasp. Otherwise, when you finally hear the answer you'll kick yourself for not thinking hard or deeply enough."

After the answer to a particularly profound Gold Star question is revealed, I always ask my students to raise their hands if they now agree that they should've indeed arrived at this answer for themselves. I want to constantly prove to them that nothing in my class is impossible; it just may take some deep, careful thought and some time.

My occasional query of "Are you all ready for a Gold Star question?" is always met with enthusiasm and my students sitting up in their seats and rubbing their hands together in anticipation of a new challenge. Rigor *can* be rousing.

Preserving Fairness

I also use encouragement by telling a student who has given me an insightful yet incomplete answer, "Oh, you're *so close* to earning the Gold Star right now! Can you give me a little bit more…? Take another moment to think, but you can see that your answer has now pointed everyone else in the right direction, and they're dying to steal this from you. The vultures are circling, but this is all yours. You just need you to go one level deeper."

If the student can't quite seize the star, I tell them that I'll come back to them at the very end if someone else doesn't give a more accurate and in-depth answer. Otherwise, students only get one shot to answer a Gold Star question. I don't have unlimited time to hear from everyone more than once. Yet if no one can come up with a correct or fully correct response, I still do not reveal the answer. I simply announce that the Gold Star is now off the table, and I give my students a series of leading questions until they themselves finally arrive at the answer. [For a wonderful way to include all students in class discussions, read Chapter 8: Embracing Fairness in *The Firm, Fair, Fascinating Facilitator* (Ward, 2015).]

Giving the Glory

When a student answers a Gold Star question correctly, I take the necessary time to point out the logic and merits of their answer. Also, I specifically refer back to other students and explain why their answers were close but did not go deep enough or why they just missed the mark.

Then, I take out my little treasure chest that contains my Gold Star stickers and ceremoniously walk over to that successful student's desk. The first page of the reader's notebooks is reserved for Gold Stars. I peel off a star and stick it onto the page as I proudly announce, "Ladies and gentlemen, _____'s first glorious Gold Star!" The entire class then erupts into applause.

Next, I instruct the celebrated student to write today's date next to the star and a sentence restating their correct answer. The reason for this is twofold: I, as well as the student, now can easily remember why they earned their star, and this documentation prevents students from going out and purchasing a package of star stickers and falsely rewarding themselves.

If while bestowing a Gold Star to a student, they ever turn to their Gold Star page and I see even one previous star already there, I gasp and shield my eyes from the blinding glare of sparkling stars as I dramatically exclaim, "Ladies and gentlemen, _____'s *second* (or whatever number) grand and glittering Gold Star!" Again, enthusiastic applause.

Sharing the Glory

You'll be pleased to see that in your fair classroom your students will root for each other's success just as much as they also compete for Gold Stars. The Gold Stars will galvanize your students like nothing you've ever experienced. Challenge is very validating.

Sometimes, if a student has only half of the answer and another student subsequently provides the full answer, ask the latter student if they mind splitting their Gold Star. You will find that kids in a Four Fs class are always very gracious, and you may even have to cut Gold Stars into thirds and fourths if a few students each contributed a vital piece of the puzzle. My students well know that some tasks take more than one person to accomplish.

Prestige is Plenty

If you're wondering what a student actually gets for earning a Gold Star, join the club because you'll receive the same questions from your students soon after the first Gold Stars are awarded. I always answer thusly: "What do you get? You mean besides the honor and the glory and the prestige and the acclaim? What greater reward could there be?" And I leave it at that.

A gold star is not an extrinsic reward; it's the formal documentation of the intrinsic reward of being the only student who accomplished an especially difficult task successfully. Those seemingly juvenile little stars will mean the world to your students, and they will be coveted and prized like you would not believe.

Preserving Honor

Something to stress to your students after every Gold Star question has been answered is: "Honor, honesty, integrity, and trust are the most important things to me. So, do not talk about what specifically happens in my class with my other students who have me during a different period. Do not ask them questions about my class, and do not tell them about my class in terms of specifically what happens in the books we are reading or concerning any discussion questions or answers, especially Gold Stars!

"It would be such a shame if a student correctly answered a difficult question, and I secretly thought to myself, *He's not smart enough to know that answer by himself... He must have gotten the answer from someone in my other class.* You would never want me to doubt your intelligence or integrity that way, so do not ask or talk about my class with any other students from another period. Remember: What happens in this period, *stays* in this period." Make this last sentence your frequent classroom chant.

If you ever do get suspicious that a student was fed an answer from a student in another period, firmly remind your class that the easiest thing for you to do to end cheating is to simply stop offering Gold Stars in this particular class. They will never want that, and students will do a good job of keeping each other honest.

Examples of Gold Star Questions

For the following questions, I'm not looking for the obvious answer. Plenty of hands will instantly fly up when I ask these questions, but the majority of these initial answers will only scratch the surface or remain at a basic comprehension level. There's more than meets the eye in all of the following questions, and it will take some serious thinking to arrive at the *real* answers.

From *Shiloh*:

- Explain what these three sets of people have in common: the people who offer Mom headache cures, the people who leave food in their mailboxes for Dad, and Mr. Wallace telling his customers that the Prestons need help.
- Explain who the *real* loser was in the deal between Marty and Judd.
- Explain the *real* reason why Marty continues to hide the truth and refuses to tell his dad about the dead doe.

From *The Watsons Go to Birmingham—1963*:

- When Kenny talks about the bus stop in chapter 2, use one word to describe Kenny.
- Explain what Byron's *real* advice is to Kenny about LJ Jones.
- Explain what Rufus is *really* doing when he turns his head and pretends not to see Kenny cry about Larry Dunn.
- Explain the *real* reason why Kenny could not deal with the Birmingham bombing.

From *Roll of Thunder, Hear My Cry*:

- If you believe that Miss Crocker is an Uncle Tom, explain what else you must then believe.
- In chapter 3, identify and explain the worst act of prejudice so far in the book.
- Explain who was *really* to blame for everything that happened to Cassie in Strawberry.
- Explain how Mr. Morrison got Uncle Hammer to give up his revenge on Mr. Simms.
- Explain what is in Mr. Jamison's mind that makes his defense of T.J. in the face of a bunch of angry nightriders so heroic.

From *The Outsiders*:

- Explain why Ponyboy waits until the end of chapter 8 to tell us that Cherry's eyes are green.

Chapter 8.

Culminating Projects

Can teachers sustain a student's enthusiasm for a recently-completed novel while also reinforcing that student's understanding of the literary elements and figurative language they've been learning?

Can teachers be certain a student actually read and understood a book on their own and simultaneously encourage that student's creativity so they begin to write like the authors they've been reading?

Ten Book Report Ideas Students Love

My middle school students achieve the literacy goals above by completing my Book Jacket Report whenever they finish reading a whole-class novel or an independent book. This engaging and scholarly assignment can easily be modified to fit the needs of elementary and high school students.

The Front Cover

This Book Jacket Report can be completely done by hand on one sheet of lined paper. Students fold their paper in half so the holes are on the bottom and the top blue margin line faces right. (This exact fold will be important later in the process.)

On the front, turned vertically, and under their name, students write their book's title but also create a brand-new title. This simple act of ingenuity yields fantastic results, often with the students devising new book titles that are superior to the original.

The rest of the front page is reserved for students to design and color a completely new and appropriate book cover for their book. Some students illustrate the most exciting, funny, or emotional part of the book. Others make their drawing more profound by adding thematic or symbolic elements to their cover art.

Inside the Book Jacket

If students fold their papers according to the format explained above, on the inside they will have a whole front side of regular lined paper onto which they can complete the following ten requirements.

1.) Protagonist/Hero: Identify the main character of the story, who the story is mainly about, or the hero.

2.) Antagonist/Enemy: Identify who or what tries to prevent the protagonist from reaching his/her goals or the villain. List as many antagonists that apply to the book.

3.) Conflict: Write all the types of conflict that apply to your book and the specific characters or things that were in conflict.

   Person vs. person/people: _____ vs. _____

   Person vs. society/most people: _____ vs. _____

   Person vs. nature: _____ vs. _____

   Person vs. something within him/herself: _____ vs. _____

4.) Genre: The type or category of a book. (Identify all that apply to your book.)

   Fiction (not a true story): mystery, adventure, horror/scary, science fiction, fantasy, romance/love story, drama/play, young adult, adult/novel, classic/award-winning, sports, humor/funny, animal story, Latino, African-American, Asian, other countries/cultures_____

   Non-fiction (a true story or factual information): biography, autobiography, historical

5.) Protagonist Metaphor: Create an original metaphor by comparing the protagonist to something unlike him/herself but that makes sense when you explain it.

   Character's Name was a _____ because _____.

   Example from *Shiloh*: Marty's life was a math book because it contained a lot of problems.

6.) Antagonist Simile: Create an original simile by using the word *like* and by comparing the antagonist to something unlike him/herself but that makes sense when you explain it.

Character's Name was like a _____ because_____.

Example from *Shiloh*: Judd was like a bag of chips because he was mostly empty and broken inside.

7.) Protagonist Alliteration: Create original alliteration (repeating the same starting letter or sound) using the character's first or last name with a word that describes the protagonist.

Example from *Shiloh*: Preston the protector (or protective Preston)

8.) Antagonist Alliteration: Create original alliteration (repeating the same starting letter or sound) using the character's first or last name with a word that describes the antagonist.

Example from *Shiloh*: Judd the jealous (or jealous Judd)

9.) Personalized License Plate: Create a personalized license plate that one character would have when they own their own car. Use a combination of up to eight letters or numbers that would make the perfect license plate for this character.

Example from *Shiloh*: HNST2DOG (Marty) or 123HUNT (Judd)

10.) My Rating: Draw and color up to five stars to rate your book. You may give half stars.

(I have my students include two more elements. They must write their book's information in proper MLA format and must correctly identify the point of view of their book.)

The Back Cover

On the back of their folded paper (turned horizontally so they have a half page of lined paper), students compose a short review and critique offering their overall opinion of the book they read. In an organized paragraph, students provide examples and evidence for what they liked or disliked about the book.

Possible positive examples: *funny, scary, exciting, interesting, emotional, touching, sad, wise, heartwarming, unpredictable, surprising, shocking, unforgettable, realistic, had great characters or lots of action.* (Students back up these examples with specific details from the book.)

Independent Reading Bookmarks

While my students are reading independently, whether in class or for homework, they add to and complete a four-page "bookmark" for each book they read. They simply staple four pieces of lined paper and fold these papers lengthwise. These long, folded pages serve as a bookmark to hold their place each time they finish reading.

These independent reading bookmarks also contain the following four components:

Page 1. Book Information

Total pages, reading level, and the book's information is written in MLA format.

Page 2. Class Vocabulary Words Seen in My Book and Page Number Evidence

I don't need to give traditional vocabulary tests. Instead, my proof that my students have learned the class vocabulary words I provide for our whole-class novels is when they can independently identify many of these same words in the books they're independently reading. In turn, this activity proves to my students that most of the words I give them are necessary and ubiquitous.

This process came about organically when many years ago my students would come to me astonished that they happened to see one of our class vocabulary words in a book they were reading on their own. I decided then to make a formal assignment out of it, and this vocabulary scavenger hunt has been as staple of my independent reading process ever since.

Page 3. Major Settings

Page 4. Important Characters, Appositives, and Page Number First Seen

Settings and character pages follow the same format as in the reader's notebook explained in Chapter 4.

***

These handy bookmarks assist my students in their comprehension of the book they're reading independently and reinforce the skills we practice in class. Completing these simple bookmarks is an organic process with students adding to their vocabulary, setting, and character pages as needed, in the same way they write these in their reader's notebooks for our whole-class novels.

Don't see any vocabulary words or new characters when you read today? No problem. Just add this evidence to your four-page independent reading bookmark the next time you see it in your book.

I use these bookmarks instead of reading logs. Because they're extremely difficult to fake, these bookmarks provide teachers with solid proof that a student both read and understood their book. Used in combination with the Book Jacket Report, teachers have a great way to assess student independent reading, and students create wonderful keepsakes of their reading journeys.

The Heroic Challenge

As an advocate of the growth and benefit mindsets, teach children that heroism doesn't require an obsession with perfection or product. When educators also value process and progress, passion and purpose, as well as putting others first and paying it forward, students are better prepared to accomplish honorable acts of their own.

Also, emphasize that heroes mostly consist of ordinary people who gallantly carry out admirable deeds—frequently in the midst of difficult situations or personal challenges. Despite inevitable shortcomings, stumbles, or setbacks, heroes ultimately rise to the occasion and selflessly help others, often simultaneously helping themselves. I call these everyday people Super-Ordinary Heroes.

In fact, the hero usually is the only person who could create such a positive outcome in a given situation. If it were not for this unique human being's cunning, courage, and compassion, the world itself would be less well off. Despite hurdles, heartache, and hardship, heroes ultimately leave themselves and humankind in a better place than when they began.

Heroism is human nature. Being a hero means remaining loving despite every reason to hate, remaining sensitive despite every reason to be cold, remaining brave despite every reason to run away, remaining peaceful despite every reason to fight, remaining forgiving despite every reason to hold a grudge or seek revenge, remaining hopeful despite every reason to despair, remaining steadfast despite every reason to give up, and remaining understanding despite every reason to judge. These are some of the major thematic lessons in the novels we read together and major contributors to how I reach the whole child.

Every hero must beware of their flaws, however, because if weaknesses are not kept in check, they can destroy the hero. Slaying dragons often is easier than controlling the negative tendencies that live inside of us all. In fact, learning from our protagonists' mistakes, as well as their triumphs, is yet another way to meet the needs of the whole child.

What Would I Do Today if I Were Brave?

Encourage students to ask themselves: *What would I do today if I were brave?* Also, teach them that true courage is not acting in the absence of fear; for how can you be brave if you aren't even scared? Rather, courage is taking action *even though* you're practically petrified with fright. Courage is also having the ability to remain calm and peaceful as you find a solution that doesn't involve hatred, violence, or revenge. Remind children that even though they want to fit in, they can also stand up for what they know is right, even if they are standing alone.

Relationships are paramount to successfully manage and educate kids, but relationships are more than just bonds of trust, belonging, and nurture; relationships are made stronger by the honest sharing and shaping of opinions, emotions, and experiences. One way a teacher can assist students in developing as a productive part of the human race is to continually couch their decisions and actions in heroic terms. Armed with the true definition of a hero, we can approach our entire lives as heroic journeys, and a specific list of what it actually looks like to be a hero helps kids along this forward path (Price-Mitchell, 2012).

A great number of children have no overriding purpose or focus in their lives, and this isn't just a problem in places of poverty. All children must have something that steers them far clear of the negative influences that are anxiously waiting to suck them in the moment kids find themselves aimless, abandoned, ambivalent, or, worse, apathetic.

Tell Heroic Stories

If preaching to children doesn't go very far, what works infinitely better is when kids can identify heroic qualities in people other than themselves. These heroes can be found in the remarkable real men and women of history. These heroes reside in every subject in school, so fascinating teachers can focus on these outstanding individuals' personal journeys. Most often, these paragons also faced challenges that would've made the best of us refuse to even try, let alone to persevere and then to succeed so greatly.

Parents and teachers need not diminish or dismiss these life lessons that are all around us. Children need to hear these stories—in their entirety, not just in their notoriety. The story behind the story is what really inspires and instructs kids about the realities of personal success and the successes that serve others as well.

When appropriate, you may also have a story of your own to recount to your students. They will eat it up! Many children look at adults, especially teachers, as capricious rewarders and punishers and people who mostly judge them instead of guiding and coaching them. Break that negative stereotype by being supremely and deeply fascinating and a collaborator in your students' growth in wisdom.

Being heroic simply means showing ourselves and others the best of what humans have to offer. We should cultivate and celebrate the hero living in each of us. Teachers can assist in this noble quest by supporting students in finding what is special about them (and each other) and in nurturing that singular gift only they each can heroically share with the world. This places further importance on students being encouraged to cultivate their talents and to pursue their individual interests that serve as the foundation for each person's personal superpowers.

Once students can identify positive, productive qualities in others—first in books, media, and history; then in friends and family—they soon recognize and develop those same advantageous attributes in themselves. Teachers who attend to the whole child understand how social-emotional-soulful learning directly impacts student success and satisfaction and actively encourage their students to become role models in their own right.

The Super-Ordinary Hero Project

Try this inspiring, interdisciplinary culminating project that works well with students at any grade level. Since kids of all ages are obsessed with superheroes, channel their natural interests into practical ways children can exemplify noble qualities that not only benefit themselves but others. According to *KQED/MindShift*, "…educators are finding that connecting projects to a global community is a powerful way to make a project feel meaningful to students" (Schwartz, 2017).

Providing Exemplars

It helps to begin the school year with a list that provides students with examples of what everyday people do to improve themselves and their surroundings. Use the following list for students to identify positive, productive qualities in literary characters, as well as in the change makers of history, science, math, sports, and the arts. Consider making this an interdisciplinary activity that also includes what students have learned in their other classes.

Even though the following list of gifts we each can bestow is extensive, it's not meant to be exhaustive. This list is instructive, but it can be illustrative as well. While it provides examples of what we each can do to improve ourselves and our communities, it can also be used to identify positive, productive qualities in others. Finding reliable role models, both real-life and fictional, is vital as we all endeavor to proceed from belief to behavior. Besides, acknowledging and appreciating the good deeds of others is yet another way of increasing our individual positive impact.

Everyday Acts of Leadership, Love, Laughter, and Learning

1. Leadership's Social Contribution

- **Stewardship of people and planet:** set an example, act as a role model, preserve and protect the natural world, treat animals humanely
- **Service to others**: help out, volunteer, practice generosity of time and resources
- **Self-awareness:** develop mindfulness, presence, self-discipline, and self-reflection
- **Steadfastness:** maintain a good reputation; exemplify trustworthiness, reliability, and responsibility; honor commitments; keep promises
- **Synergy:** personify nonviolence, respect, patience, calm, and cooperation; build bridges; play fairly
- **Solutions:** apologize, forgive, make amends, find connections and common ground, think win-win, seek justice and equity

2. Love's Emotional Advantage

- **Empathy:** embody kindness, consideration, concern, and understanding; put yourself in others' shoes

- **Inclusion:** embrace tolerance; celebrate difference; honor individuality; offer welcome; demonstrate acceptance, warmth, and courtesy
- **Encouragement:** provide support, cheer, and reassurance; calm and console others
- **Interaction:** communicate, let people in, actively listen
- **Openness:** practice sincerity and honesty, express your feelings
- **Affection:** extend friendship, display loyalty, exhibit faithfulness, show devotion, offer trust, act with love and tenderness
- **Attention:** embrace sensitivity, be attuned to others' needs, be accessible
- **Optimism:** search for the positive, cling to hope, look on the bright side
- **Assurance:** display confidence and humility, advocate for yourself, speak up and speak out

3. Laughter's Soulful Legacy

- **Passion:** pursue aspirations; express enthusiasm and ambition; practice authenticity; share your dreams, desires, and delights; follow your heart
- **Play:** value experiences over things, revel in wonder, embrace adventure, commune with nature, explore, experiment, inspire, laugh out loud and often
- **Panache:** make art, create beauty, pursue creativity, flaunt a personal style
- **Pluck:** try new things, trust your instincts, exhibit bravery and gallantry, live your convictions, go against the crowd, stand up for what is right
- **Purpose:** search for meaning, honor the past, live in the present
- **Profundity:** look below the surface, slow down, savor the moment, embrace mystery and the unknown, reveal interconnectedness
- **Praise:** practice gratitude, appreciate others

4. Learning's Intellectual and Practical Value

- **Wisdom:** learn from mistakes, keep improving and refining
- **Well-Read and Well-Informed:** know history, keep up with current events, think critically, ask questions, fall in love with reading
- **With It-ness:** invest in preparation and organization, plan ahead, exercise caution, identify and access resources, ask for assistance and opinions

- **Work:** become a self-starter, practice diligence, honor duty, take pride in a job well done, employ calculated effort to work smarter rather than harder
- **Willpower:** develop drive, determination, and dedication; expect struggles, stumbles, and setbacks; embrace challenge
- **Weathering Storms:** be resilient, bounce back from mistakes and bad luck

Be sure to add to this list throughout the school year as more heroic qualities and positive theme category examples are found and while students learn about the famous and not-so-famous folk who populate your subject area. It's wise to also point out the flaws and bad decisions these people make because no one is, or must be, perfect. In fact, life and literature are filled with those who made mistakes and experienced misfortune. Nevertheless, these heroes eventually redeemed themselves and overcame obstacles so they could both better themselves and the world.

After spending the school year identifying and discussing the positive traits of others, students can focus on how they themselves can exemplify similar heroic qualities. Students create an avatar (something visual used to also represent non-visual concepts or ideas) for themselves that they call their Super-Ordinary Hero.

Each student decides how to bring their hero to life. In order to represent their heroic self, students may choose to make a poster, a large doll, a booklet, a diorama, a mobile, a comic book, a film (live-action or animated), a multimedia presentation, etc. Creativity and originality are part of the fun!

The following items are some of the components you can require your students to include in their project. Feel free to add to this basic list, and encourage student suggestions as well. Remind students that the hero they create is an amalgamation of not only who they currently are but who they aspire to be.

The Components of a Super-Ordinary Hero

Heroic Nickname: Every superhero needs a special name, so students create an appropriate nickname that broadly defines all the good they do for themselves and others. Students may use alliteration for their heroic name.

My heroic nickname would be The Fascinating Philosopher because I enjoy sharing the wisdom I have learned with my students, as well as hearing the insights and opinions they have discovered on their own and with my support in the books we've read together.

Motto: Maybe we cannot leap tall buildings in a single bound, but an inspiring rallying cry, slogan, or catchphrase succinctly captures a hero's main objectives or assets. Students create a motto that gives their life direction and purpose.

My heroic motto would be: "With a great book in hand, the Fascinating Philosopher influences the future by touching hearts and awakening minds."

Outfit: Even though the point is for students to rouse the everyday hero inside of themselves, every superhero needs a special get-up or costume to show the world exactly what they stand for. Have students draw, dress, or delineate their noble garb.

My heroic outfit would definitely include a cape made from the repurposed pages of the beloved books that over time have naturally fallen apart at the hands of scores of eager student readers.

Symbol: Whether this visual representation of each student's heroism is emblazoned on their outfit or it decorates their shield, cape, or headgear, this insignia encapsulates who each student strives to be. Students also write a short explanation for their symbol.

My heroic symbol would be an apple tree because this represents teaching, growth, deep roots, nature, and knowledge.

Gear: Please emphasize peace and positivity as students select their heroic accouterments. Weapons and items of violence and destruction have no place in this project. Super-Ordinary Heroes are defenders of justice and champions of kindness, who are less interested in battling evil and more intent on spreading goodwill and doing good deeds.

My hero's gear would consist of my trusty handkerchief to dry my eyes when something especially moving happens in my classroom, my reading glasses so I can respond to my students' remarkable writing, and my wristwatch so I can monitor the pace and flow of each engaging lesson.

Vehicle: Every hero has their favored mode of transportation, preferably one that is eco-friendly. Students not only draw or describe their vehicle, they also create a personalized license plate that consists of up to eight letters or numbers.

My hero's vehicle would be my wheeled desk chair that enables me to roll from student to student and to converse with them at their level. My vehicle's license plate would read: EYE2EYE.

Headquarters: Students create a home base for their hero. Whether it is their current bedroom or the home of their dreams, students show or describe the environment that enables them to reflect, recharge, and recreate.

My heroic headquarters is my fantasy classroom with large sunny windows that look out upon a thriving student garden.

Super-Ordinary Powers: While aspects of these heroic personas are aspirational, they're also grounded firmly in the real world. Students use the heroic qualities from the classroom master list to select their top three choices from each of the four categories of Leadership, Love, Laughter, and Learning (Ward, 2016). Students may feature more than three heroic characteristics for each category, but caution them not to get hung up on having to do it all. Every impact matters—and matters more than we may ever know. Students must also explain why each quality is personally meaningful, as well as how they specifically plan to exemplify or implement each quality in the future.

Influential Actions: This is where students take what they've learned in all of their classes and specifically recount the gallant deeds of the people from literature, history, science, mathematics, etc. Students compose at least four short narratives that describe the caring, courageous actions of the people they've been studying and who they most admire.

Words of Wisdom: Students directly quote the words and writing of the people they have learned about. These can be short quotations from the same people whose influential actions were related above, or they can be from additional people and books from this year's lessons.

Achilles Heel/Kryptonite: We all have our flaws, our weaknesses, and our lapses. It's important to be aware of our foibles so we do not become our own worst enemy or inadvertently hurt others. Students self-reflect and honestly explain their three greatest shortcomings or temptations that sometimes get in the way of being their best.

One of my Achilles heels is imbalance. As long as I equally attend to my students' social, emotional, soulful, academic, and altruistic needs, they will move forward. I also must steer clear of giving up on any student, especially when they have already given up on themselves. In addition, haste always makes waste in a classroom, and I must honor process and progress just as much as product and performance.

Chapter 9.

Collaboration, Inquiry, and Feedback

Any teacher who wishes to have their students interact and work together must keep in mind four overarching aspects of collaborative learning:

1. The Group Work Litmus Test

A good test for whether group work is even necessary for a particular assignment is this: *After you've provided your students with the essential knowledge and skills, if the vast majority can successfully complete an assignment while working individually, with very little teacher assistance, then no group or partner work is needed.*

It's as simple as that.

Just because students like to work together and it seems to make things easier to pacify them, those are not enough justification for group work. Just because it may appear to some that you're a super teacher because your students are perpetually seated in groups, that in and of itself is not a good reason for collaborative learning. In fact, these weak rationales for group work will probably backfire on you.

You must have very specific reasons for your students to collaborate on any given assignment. These justifications must satisfy your own scrutiny, as well as that of parents and administrators, who are looking for a challenging, meaningful learning experience for every student—not merely a free-for-all where groups of students chatter away while individually completing an assignment that never necessitated their classmates' assistance or input in the first place.

Similarly, if it makes your life easier to have your more attentive (not necessarily more skilled) students re-teach to their lackadaisical partners what all students should easily have been able to grasp on their own had they been focused during direct instruction, then you're allowing your more conscientious students to "enable" inattention in others, which only makes the problem continue. You are even allowing those mindful students' learning time to be wasted in helping others who clearly are not helping themselves.

True group work is not about students merely helping each other or re-teaching; it's a synergistic process that yields a product greater than the sum of its parts. Interconnections, interdependence, sharing of strengths, and working towards a common goal are all components of true collaboration (*ResourcEd*, 2017).

Nonetheless, be honest and prudent about how ready both you and your students are for serious, successful group work. Re-examine the assignments you've planned for group work, and make certain they pass this simple litmus test. Also, re-assess if your classroom management during direct instruction and individual class work is functioning to your satisfaction. If not, sharpen your management skills before launching into group work. Group work that is well planned and well executed is always worth the wait!

(It's acknowledged that sometimes group work is logistically necessary. If you only have a limited number of books, manipulatives, microscopes, etc. then sharing the wealth is the only choice. Nevertheless, seize this necessity for cooperation as an opportunity for you to also incorporate some collaborative component. "Fuller, richer, and deeper" should always be the words to guide your lesson planning for groups.)

2. Collaborative, Not Cooperative, Groupings

Note the distinction between "collaborative" and "cooperative" learning. Of course, cooperation is a cornerstone of any teacher's game plan and is always occurring in a well-functioning classroom, but actual *collaboration* is the hallmark of legitimate group work.

Therefore, if a task doesn't absolutely necessitate two or more students working closely together, where each individual is contributing an *equal, necessary, and vital element* to the end product and where two or more minds are achieving something much greater than one individual could produce on their own, then just leave that particular assignment to the individual.

Instead, save your most demanding, profound, and altruistic assignments for groups. You'll have much better management and academic results with groups when your students are deeply involved in a truly daunting and important task. Greatly reduce your students' opportunity and temptation to socialize or fade out by only assigning them something serious and compelling to accomplish during those instances when you give them the well-earned privilege and excitement of collaborating with their peers.

3. Complexity is King for Group Work

Students need a reason to collaborate, and that reason always comes from complexity. The distraction, jabber, and bickering that can occur when students work with each other often stem from the lack of complexity of the assignment itself.

There used to be a teacher axiom to "keep students so busy, they don't have time to fool around." While mindless worksheets and endless busywork are thankfully things of the past, there's a grain of truth in that old adage. If we substitute the word *engaged* for the word *busy*, we can see the motivational power that meaningful assignments engender.

The real reason to collaborate is because a task is intricate and sophisticated; it's too difficult and has too many pieces to complete alone. Approached in the right way, every student will rise to a challenge—as long as that challenge is deemed worthy of their effort, students have some choice in the matter, and they have some stake in the outcome.

This is why project-based and problem-based learning are perfect for fruitful group work. Add deep passion and a greater purpose to PBL, and your students' engagement will transform into investment!

4. Prepare Students to be Good Team Members

According to Sweeney (2010), there are seven Ps for students to follow when working collaboratively:

Pausing, paraphrasing, and probing are great ways to extend collaborative conversations. Teachers use these techniques all the time during class discussions, so have your students mirror these same talking techniques while working together.

Putting ideas on the table is the logical result of productive student conversations. Without the first three Ps, students won't have the benefit of every member's full participation and thoughts. Strive for equal, integral input from each group member.

Paying attention to oneself and others and presuming positive intentions both require the self-awareness and respect that ensure group work is serious and rewarding. Those petty student arguments so common in other classrooms won't occur in a setting of mutual courtesy and cooperation.

Pursuing a balance between advocacy and inquiry entails that students truly want to collaborate. If there are students who are fixated on seeing that only their ideas and their input are ultimately used, then why collaborate in the first place?

***

It should now be even more apparent how a whole-child approach must work cohesively in order to attain its maximum effect. *Classroom management* does matter when you expect your students to collaborate effectively, respectfully, and responsibly. *Student confidence* and a sense of trust and belonging are indeed crucial when students are expected to open up and share their ideas with each other. A *profound sense of passion and purpose* are certainly vital when students are expected to work on large, ongoing, complex projects. A *strong skillset* is absolutely requisite when you expect students to perform successfully, especially when the completion of their passion project affects the others in their collaborative group. Finally, a *sense of contributing essentially* is paramount when you expect perseverance and integrity from your students.

High expectations are one thing, but implementing the strategies that empower your students to progressively meet and eventually exceed your high expectations is what transforms aspirations into actualities.

Inquiry Puts Students in Charge of Learning

We say we want students to move past surface information as they deeply study and even read between the lines of challenging text, but how do we support them to independently interact with a variety of texts in a variety of subjects? As always, the answer is to be found in a balanced approach to teaching. We must value teacher modeling and direct instruction, right along with progressively putting students in charge of their own learning and with the teacher acting as a facilitator.

Because we provide students with an increasingly challenging, rich curriculum and assignments throughout the school year, every student will rely on and find comfort in a teacher who also strategically guides the class whenever complexity is heightened. As we help students progress, several scaffolds, strategies, and systems are steadily provided and continuously practiced. At the same time, teachers offer students opportunities to ponder, create, and hypothesize all on their own or with partners. Of course, the dance between a teacher being hands-on and hands-off is one that varies from class to class and from student to student. Again, the key is finding equilibrium. A great teacher is neither too didactic nor too *laissez faire*.

The Inquiry Approach

Allowing your students to create their own text-based questions suddenly gives structure to the often-mysterious skills of analysis and inference. Breaking down the inquiry process into two basic types of questions allows students to show off what they know, what they uncovered, and what they surmised as evidenced by their comprehension and interpretation of the text.

A student may not know everything about a text, but they certainly must prove they know some things that are structural, significant, and sublime. If students can pose thoughtful questions that prove they analyzed, understood, and made some inferences about the text, this is as valid an assessment of these skills as any quiz, essay, or simple summary.

In addition, require your students to write answers for their own questions written in complete sentences and using evidence from the text as their proof. This evidence can either be paraphrased using the student's own words or written as a formal citation/quotation from the text, depending on which skill you want them to practice. In either case, at minimum always have students note the page number from where they found their evidence, using parenthesis at the end of their evidence.

Be sure to have students write their questions and answers on *two separate sheets of paper* because they will be challenging their classmates to answer their questions later in this process. This process as explained here works best with students working collaboratively with single partners, rather than in larger collaborative groups. Both partners come to consensus in creating and answering questions, and each partner writes the exact same questions and answers on their own two sheets of paper.

Alongside each answer, students must also indicate if they mostly used their comprehension of the text or had to make an inference about the text in order to answer their own question. It's important for students to clearly realize when an answer can be found directly in the text ("right there") and when they're "reading between the lines" in order to make an inference. If an inference was necessary, students must include an explanation sentence in order to link their reasoning with evidence from the text.

You can leave the creation of questions to your students' individual discretion but always require them to create a minimum number of questions, with a balance between comprehension and inference questions.

Providing Support

Even as I continually model probing questions during class discussions, my students are often overwhelmed with creating their own questions for a large piece of text, and some need specific direction for where to begin. For the students who need more structure, I give them a menu of choices or assign specific topics for which to create their questions. For narrative and some history texts, I often assign pairs of students to focus on one character, person, chapter, scene, or event.

For informational, argumentative, and science texts, you can assign a certain concept, chapter, section, page, etc. for students to base their questions on. This sort of chunking gives students direction and is another way for you to differentiate your instruction according to your individual students' current skill levels and needs.

As their facilitator, assist those students who are truly lost. Give them the guidance to become a self-starter and a way to focus in on what they currently understand. This "showing off what you know" aspect of the inquiry process is another aspect of teacher fairness because you emphasize to your students that right now they're focusing only upon what they're sure they know or can reasonably assume about the text. You will of course step in later to clear up any parts that the class still seems unclear about. Better yet, when students soon have a chance to interact with their other classmate's questions, those gaps may be filled organically.

Advanced students need a facilitator, too. Be sure to push these students to dig deeper, to think more critically, to make connections, and to uncover patterns.

Answering a Classmate's Questions

After student pairs have finished creating their questions and have provided sufficient answers for their own questions on two separate pieces of paper, have them *partner with a different classmate and only trade their question papers*. Caution students not to allow their new partner to see their answer paper. Each student independently answers all of their second partner's text-based questions on a new, separate, third piece of paper. Emphasize to the class that all questions will continue to be answered in complete sentences, along with the appropriate textual evidence and/or explanation.

Students sit next to this new partner while they're answering each other's questions, but each student is now working independently. It's still helpful for students to be next to each other, however, in case their new partner has any problems with reading or understanding their questions. If so, students may clarify for them.

Critical Thinking—Evaluate and Explain

When finished with answering each other's questions, students give back their second partner's questions paper and also give them the answer paper they just wrote. Next, they *return to their original partner* and together evaluate the answer papers that their second partners just wrote and gave to them. The original partners now compare and contrast those two answer papers with the original answers they both had written.

For each answer, each student comes to consensus with their original partner and explains whether their first answer, one of their two other classmate's answers, or a combination of two or three of the answers in front of them provides the most complete and correct answer to each of their questions. As always, students are respectful and supportive when they evaluate their classmates' answers. Each partner writes their evaluations on a fourth piece of paper.

Processes like this inquiry approach differentiate the learning of each student, while also allowing all students to fully interact with the same grade-level text as their classmates. Students feel empowered by the control they're given over their own learning and enthusiastically rise to the occasion!

One powerful way to honor the student inquiry process is to create a quiz that's based entirely on the best student-generated questions gathered from all of your classes. Not only do students get to take charge of their learning, they also get to control how that learning is sometimes assessed.

Academic Feedback that Works

The following feedback template is a means to move all students progressively forward, no matter their current level of proficiency. Every student, from developing to advanced, should be focused on growth and expansion, so formative feedback is always essential (Nicol and MacFarlane-Dick, 2007).

The problem is, most academic feedback is not meaningful and contains no way to tell if students even understand it. Many teachers have no system in place to ensure that students both read and heed their advice. Because the feedback a teacher may have taken great pains to provide may merely be in the form of marks or comments on exams and essays, they're too often given no more than a cursory glance—especially by the students who need this feedback the most!

Even in the cases when students understand teacher feedback, they rarely internalize it; they neither use it as a means for improvement for the assignment at hand nor as a method for future advancement. Do any of your students endlessly repeat the same mistakes you had already pointed out to them?

Because most teacher feedback is summative rather than formative, most students simply focus on the product or the final the grade, not on the learning process or their academic progress. Whether satisfied with the end result or not, students usually view their grade on a particular assignment or exam as final, which actually may be what the teacher wants them to think.

In these cases, why would teachers then be surprised when their students couldn't care less about those tedious teacher remarks on their papers? Furthermore, why are we surprised when it seems like most parents are more fixated on grades rather than growth?

To truly be effective, feedback must be interactive, not simply face-to-face. Providing feedback aloud and in the moment is good, but synergy is so much better. Think of this one-on-one time as less of a conference and more of an equal *conversation* between author and audience.

Feedback must also be ongoing. Focusing equally on process, progress, and product, break major assignments and projects into steps or drafts. Then build in structured time to provide formative feedback at each of these important junctures. Providing ongoing feedback capitalizes on what's good and catches what's not so good so that each succeeding step shows improvement.

By the time students reach the final step or draft, your summative assessment of their work should reflect each student's best effort and achievement. Imagine how parents will feel when their child's performance is truly based on their best because it was fully supported every step of the way!

A Three-Pronged, Interactive Process

Student writers have a built-in audience right in their classrooms. They can receive feedback from their teacher and their peers, as well as from themselves in the form of self-reflection or self-assessment. Employ the following feedback triad in this order:

First, each student receives feedback from at least one of their peers. Teachers can step in and strategically pair students by varying levels of ability. This intentional, heterogeneous pairing prevents two developing students from potentially being limited in the depth and quality of feedback they could offer each other.

If you allow all students to self-select their next partner for a second round of peer feedback, however, this now allows two advanced students to pair up. Nevertheless, with the right coaching, modeling, and practice, your supposedly "low" students will soon offer astute, scholarly feedback to their (supposedly) more advanced classmates.

Next, have students individually use the same Applaud, Advise, and Advance process outlined below in order to self-reflect upon their work. As they revise or reform their work, students should draw their own conclusions about their performance, while also incorporating the peer feedback they received.

Finally, students should receive the same type of formative feedback from their teacher based on the student's second draft or subsequent revisions. This way, the teacher reviews each student's work at a juncture when the good has already been expanded upon, the most glaring mistakes have been rectified, and the opportunities for enrichment have already been explored and implemented.

Of course, the teacher has been there all along, checking in with each student, monitoring all the peer editing and self-evaluation going on, as well as being available for individual support and assistance.

Also, by conducting these teacher-student feedback sessions in person and in the moment, teachers can attend to the needs of the whole child. Relationships are strengthened, trust is solidified, and confidence is built through these very personal interchanges that are progress-driven.

Teachers can pinpoint problems or suggest strategies and send a student right back to their desk to make improvements on the spot. Then, when the student returns several minutes later, enthusiastically clutching their latest brilliant edit or astute addition that further transformed their work, the teacher can celebrate the growth right then and there, all while witnessing the pride on the student's face.

This process leaves nothing to chance. Students are finally held accountable for not only their understanding but for actually *using* the feedback they receive. Parents will see vast improvements, with potentials realized and limits stretched.

The Three As of Meaningful Formative Feedback

The following three-part process employs a simple but effective method to achieve the main goals of formative feedback. It isn't necessary to provide feedback for every aspect outlined under each of the Applaud, Advise, and Advance categories, but every feedback session must include at least one example for each of the Three As.

During a feedback session, each student sits with an editor, either a classmate or the teacher. The editor never writes upon the author's paper or work, however. This leaves the author's work pristine and ready for additional, unbiased feedback from other editors. The editor simply reads or reviews the entire work and then provides *oral feedback* in three areas.

This holistic reading or review or the student's work allows the editor to comment on and fully explain the aspects that most stood out for them. Editors are free to offer additional feedback or even to interrupt their reading or review of the work to make a particularly poignant comment or to ask clarifying questions, but generally, editors should focus on the most grand and glaring aspects of the work.

Meanwhile, it's the student author who does the writing by transcribing their editors' comments onto a separate page of Feedback Notes. Each author must write a minimum of one explanation sentence for each of the Three As, examples for which are provided below.

After the author writes each explanation provided by their editor, they must read the sentence back to the editor to ensure both accuracy and understanding. If an editor offers multiple comments or suggestions for any of the Three As, it's the author who will tell the editor which single suggestion to explain. This puts the author in the driver's seat as they choose the feedback that's most useful to them, all without being overwhelmed by an onslaught of comments or corrections.

As part of the feedback session between student and teacher, the student can provide the teacher with their Feedback Notes to ensure that the previous peer feedback was indeed incorporated into their work correctly. These Feedback Notes are also excellent artifacts for parent and student-led conferences. This way, parents can see the extent and depth of how you establish an environment of both peer and teacher support tailored just for their child. [Read my book, *Talented Teachers, Empowered Parents, Successful Students* (Ward, 2017), for an abundance of practical strategies to include parents as allies in their child's education.]

1. Applaud

Editors always begin with the positive. They search for the best features of the assignment and specifically recognize them. This capitalizes on what is already working or improving and also serves as a reminder and reinforcement of effective approaches. Every student must see that academic success doesn't come solely from innate intelligence or by sheer effort but from the implementation of effective strategies.

By specifically delineating effective strategies, students collect a wealth of methods they can continuously employ to expand upon their achievements. Editors will consult with the author for *one* positive example below to define or describe.

Marvelous: Identify particularly good aspects of the work.

Explanation: _____ *is marvelous because* _____.

Memorable: Identify remarkably creative, original, or inventive aspects of the work.

Explanation: _____ *is memorable because* _____.

Meaningful: Identify especially profound aspects of the work.

Explanation: _____ *is meaningful and deep because* _____.

Moving: Identify emotional and inspiring aspects of the work.

Explanation: _____ *is moving because* _____.

2. Advise

Next, editors focus on the nuts and bolts of the assignment. They identify what went wrong, what was overlooked, or what needs to be changed in order to make the assignment more correct, complete, or clear.

This part of the feedback process may indeed be picky or technical, but editors only concentrate on the instances when errors or omissions interfere with the full success of the assignment. Editors will consult with the author for *one* example below to fix. (If there are no mistakes, editors may proceed to step 3.)

Mistakes to avoid: Identify any errors, and choose one example to correct.

Explanation: *Avoid* _____ *so that* _____.

Missing items to add: Identify missing items, and choose one example to correct.

Explanation: *Add* _____ *in order to* _____.

Modifications to make: Identify changes, and choose one example to recommend.

Explanation: *Consider changing _____ in order to _____.*

Misperceptions to clarify or correct: Identify inconsistencies and confusions, and choose one example to recommend.

Explanation: *Consider clarifying/correcting _____ because _____.*

3. Advance

Finally, editors offer insightful, intelligent additions that could enhance the work. The type of profound thinking required for these suggestions benefits not only the work being examined but the editors themselves. Such perceptive analysis will in turn inspire peer editors to examine their own work in a much more expansive, thoughtful, and thorough manner. Editors will consult with the author for *one* suggestion below.

Move beyond: Offer specific suggestions for how to extend the conversation or information with additional ideas or analysis. Help the author stretch their limits.

Explanation: *Consider moving the conversation or your ideas forward by _____.*

Create or construct something new to add to your work, like _____.

Move below: Offer specific suggestions for how to go deeper or to read between the lines with additional insights or inference.

Explanation: *Perhaps move a level deeper by _____.*

Consider enhancing your conclusions or making informed predictions, such as _____.

Move inward: Offer specific suggestions for exploring similar ideas, situations, and facts by asking for personal opinions and experiences or for proposing new options. Encourage the author to use introspection and to bring a personal touch to their work.

Explanation: *Try making your ideas more personal by _____.*

Consider commenting on, critiquing, or thinking critically about your work, such as _____.

Move across: Offer specific suggestions for how to expose possible patterns, interconnections, or alternatives to the work.

Explanation: *Think about making a connection to _____.*

Consider comparing or contrasting what you have said with _____.

Chapter 10.

Writing with Passion and Purpose

As I explain in my book *Teaching the Benefit Mindset: Moving Empathy, Inclusion, and Altruism to the Forefront of Education* (Ward, 2018), I've reexamined my definition of the whole child. I'd always thought my particular definition was actually more expansive than most because I include the *soulful* needs of children. I knew early on that focusing solely on social-emotional and academic needs wasn't adequate, and the current emphasis on student engagement has proven to me that this fourth, deeply personal and profound component of the whole child's soulful needs was indeed vital.

I also advocate for a sense of purpose as one important facet of a child's soulful development, but now I believe one's personal purpose must also encompass a purpose greater than oneself. An increasing number of parents and educators agree, and there are many institutions solely dedicated to helping people find meaningful direction in their lives (*KQED Mind/Shift*, 2018).

Infusing the Benefit Mindset into the Whole Child

Teachers can readily agree that we want to embolden and equip every child with the knowledge and skills to become the best they can be. Yet once I learned about the benefit mindset, several questions began to surface and refused to go away:

- Is a self-confidence that is solely based on oneself and doesn't consider how one affects and interacts with others a belief system reliable enough to see one through every adversity?

- Is self-satisfaction alone sufficient for a truly full and rich life?

- Is self-efficacy and individual accomplishment enough, or is it incumbent upon educators and parents to redefine the meaning of success?

- Are we unconsciously causing today's children to become self-centered, even self-obsessed, and unintentionally creating a sense of entitlement that's not only off-putting but detrimental to the common good?

- Can our social structures and our planet itself weather unmitigated quests for self-interested acquisition and advancement?

The benefit mindset is thinking caring thoughts about all people and the whole planet. But living the benefit mindset doesn't remain only in our minds. We can actually do things that help others and protect nature. These acts of kindness create a better world for everyone (*Edutopia*, 2018a).

The benefit mindset asks each person to share what we know, what we can do, and what we can give. We don't have to know or give everything in order to help others or to make positive change. We don't even have to be experts to begin helping and adding to the wellbeing of others. The protagonists of all of the novels and films referred to in this book certainly show how even orphans, outsiders, outcasts, and underdogs can affect lasting change, both personally and collectively.

The benefit mindset adds purpose and meaning to our lives because we feel more connected to others. We also feel like our lives matter and that we truly make a difference (*Education Week*, 2018).

Communication is Key

As I wrote in my article for *Edutopia* (2018b), the longer I teach, the more I realize my rapport with each student is based on how effectively I speak with them, both publicly and one on one. When I express empathy, my students' thoughts, feelings, and experiences are validated. Through my words of warmth and acceptance, each child becomes an integral part of our class community—a community of learners, leaders, and liaisons who exemplify the benefit mindset.

I don't just talk *to* my students, however. I also value the casual conversations and academic discussions we share. No matter how some students may hide it, all kids long to be heard and understood. The best teachers listen more than they speak.

Yet no one can hear a student if the class is a chaotic cacophony. Children won't open up and share if they don't trust that their teacher and classmates are truly on their side. Kids have no impetus to reveal their passions and dreams if they find no connection to what they're learning. Students have no coherent or scholarly means of speech if they lack the support and strategies to express themselves clearly and accurately. And no one is willing to help anyone else, certainly not a stranger, if empathy and altruism are absent from daily learning and living.

Yet giving students voice isn't only about opportunity. It's also about inspiring and empowering them to speak with insight and poise. With practice, encouragement, and assistance, what students have to say can be astute and profound.

Identifying the Impact of Words

Words have power. Therefore, students must measure their words because the right choice could change someone's life, perhaps one's own. Being articulate is one of the most important skills a person can possess, and eloquence is one of the greatest gifts a teacher can bestow upon their students.

To this end, consistently point out the effects that words, both spoken and written, create. Emphasize that words are rarely neutral. The right words will probably do the job, but the wrong words will always work against you. Then allow students themselves to identify when words:

- Heal or hurt, soothe or enrage,
- Clearly explain or further confuse,
- Change minds or harden hearts,
- Bridge divides or cement separation,
- Enthrall or bore, charm or repel, or
- Move people to action or to tears.

When students analyze the dialogue in narrative texts, as well as in historical speeches, political debates, TED Talks, and tweets related what they're learning, have them also explain when word choice had a particularly significant impact. If that impact was unintentionally negative, allow collaborative groups to reword key phrases and passages and share their improvements with the class. Through this modeling and awareness of "a way with words," students' writing and personal interactions become increasingly sophisticated and nuanced.

In preparing our children to be global citizens who exemplify the benefit mindset, we need to also equip them with the social skills and tact that being well spoken provides. Developing each student's speaking, listening, and writing skills prepares children to communicate their ideas, passions, and empathy to a world that needs their unique voices and visions.

Writing is a particularly effective means of communication because it affords the writer the time and thought to communicate with precision. Writing is also very therapeutic as the writer carefully processes their thoughts and feelings into a structure that is as comprehensible as it is creative.

This chapter offers several innovative ways for students to cultivate and share the benefit mindset through writing. Not only will your students' literacy skills improve in general; your students will become much better thinkers, advocates, and leaders via the written word.

The Good News

Assigning students to read and write about current events has been a staple of learning in most subject areas. However, much of the news today consists of reports about scandals, crimes, violence, disasters, and dire predictions.

Why not use the benefit mindset to counter all that negativity, no matter how "real" that negativity may be? Try assigning students to scour the week's news for stories of progress, invention, hope, and humanitarianism. Filling your learning environment with such promise and positivity inspires your students to focus on creative solutions and how we all can give back and move others forward.

Students can share with the class the remarkable strides that individuals and institutions are making across the globe. Some stories may even become ongoing studies of the continued advances these people and programs make, as well as how they employ a growth mindset to deal with unexpected challenges and overcome setbacks.

A barrage of negativity often discourages people from even trying. This doesn't mean we shield children from the inhumanity and pain of the past and present because, as we've seen, many novels frankly deal with tragedies, both real and imagined.

But we don't have to dwell on such doom and gloom either. Instead, we can acknowledge the bad, while we intentionally focus on those who strove to do good. Some of these upstanders may have succeeded in righting wrongs, and some may have fallen short, both privately and publically. But if we want children to begin living the benefit mindset, we can teach them to look to those who have paved the way of empathy, inclusion, and altruism.

Envisioning Utopia

In the *Time* article "Paradise Lost: The Mysterious Case of the Missing Utopian Novels," Sarah Begely (2017) asks why "pessimistic fiction has thrived in recent years." Educators have certainly seen the rise of young adult novels set in a decidedly dystopian future. While such novels are rife with conflict and drama, one benefit of these popular books is they teach kids that they can triumph over any obstacle. These books also serve as cautionary tales about how authoritarianism and technology must be kept in check.

But like the negative news reports that teachers can help balance out with a concentration on the Good News, teachers can also ask students to write their own narratives set in a decidedly utopian future, a future that could be realized within their own lifetime. Rather than writing a pure fantasy or a story that couldn't possibly happen for generations, students can expand upon the hopeful realities they've actually seen around them and studied in the world at large.

The Global Goals for Sustainable Development, developed by TeachSDGs (2018), are a great resource for students to envision a better world and to pinpoint where they would like to see improvements in their world:

1. No poverty
2. Zero hunger
3. Good health and wellbeing
4. Quality education
5. Gender equity
6. Clean water and sanitation
7. Affordable and clean energy
8. Decent work and economic growth
9. Industry, innovation, and infrastructure
10. Reduced inequalities
11. Sustainable cities and communities
12. Responsible consumption and production
13. Climate action
14. Life below water
15. Life on land
16. Peace and justice

Besides describing this peaceful place where a benefit mindset is the norm, students can still add elements of turmoil and suspense to their utopian story. Practicing the benefit mindset doesn't guarantee a life free from strife or struggle—not within oneself, not interpersonally, and not in regards to the changes and challenges life itself presents us with. There will always be plenty of real drama to occupy our minds and fictional conflict to entertain our thoughts, but imagining a significantly better world shows kids that this dream is absolutely within our grasp—and that we each can play a part in making such a world an imminent reality.

My Legacy

Students write a short speech they hope a close friend or family member would give for them at their 100th birthday party. This is each student's chance to document the milestones, accomplishments, and personal qualities that someone else would want to pay tribute to for a life well lived. Emphasize to students that along with references to their possible wealth or fame, the really impactful parts of the speech will focus on the specific ways they've brightened or improved the lives of others over the last hundred years.

Having children consider how they would like to be remembered far into the future and how their lives could touch others in meaningful ways allows them to envision the personal rewards to be reaped from a lifetime of living the benefit mindset.

Character Therapy

We're living in an increasingly trauma-filled world, where even the planet itself is crying out and unable to bear its stressors. "Data shows that more than half of all U.S. children have experienced some kind of trauma in the form of abuse, neglect, violence, or challenging household circumstances—and 35 percent of children have experienced more than one type of traumatic event, according to the Centers for Disease Control and Prevention" (Minero, 2017).

With teen suicides and school shootings on the rise, educators are searching for interventions for students at risk of taking lives—both their own and others'—as well as for ways to prevent troubled youth from becoming maladjusted adults who also take lives. This cycle of hopelessness and hurt must end, but how do we teach all students to be resilient, especially those who have undergone severe trauma?

One answer has been with us all along…

Stories are one way humankind passes down wisdom for dealing with life's greatest challenges. In fact, CEO Jeff Bezos has replaced PowerPoint presentations at Amazon with narrative memos because our brains are hardwired to respond to personal stories above all else (Gallo, 2018).

Young adult literature is particularly masterful at evoking empathy for people seemingly different than oneself and for equipping kids to navigate life's joys and sorrows. Such books routinely deal with deep, dark issues and provide the proper forum to discuss a whole range of problems no child should ever have to deal with—but too often do.

A *60 Minutes* report (2018) about overcoming childhood trauma taught me the power of simply asking, "What happened to you?" when dealing with a child who is chronically acting out. Instead of leaping to the indictment of "What've you done now?!" the emphasis becomes one of understanding and healing.

With this new perspective, I now allow my students to become "character therapists" and give voice to literary characters' suffering and confusion. No one gets hurt when students act as armchair psychologists for fictional characters. Rather, those students who themselves are dealing with their own trauma can find affinity and viable strategies by talking characters through their hardships, even if those struggles may differ from their own. As for the students who have no major personal issues, facilitating Character Therapy instills in them the skills anyone needs when times are tough and empowers all students with the knowledge of how they can help when others are in emotional distress.

Instead of always working from the inside out (*me*-focused), we can also have kids work from the outside in, the We in me. A focus on others through empathy and altruism also teaches us understanding and kindness for ourselves.

The Character Therapy Process

For this project, students write a dialogue between themselves and a character who has undergone severe stress. Students can interact with the story by adding probable details and situations that may have only been hinted at in the book. The point isn't for students to sensationalize what characters have endured; it's to respectfully put themselves in the shoes of their chosen character and to give expanded voice to their experiences.

As I wrote for *Edutopia* (2018c), here's the four-step process that guides students in writing effective Character Therapy dialogues:

1. Speaking Truth

Students allow the character to experience the calm of release and comfort of empathy by describing whatever happened that troubles them. Students can be taught to handle delicate issues with the proper sensitivity and seriousness, and this maturity will help them in real life conversations.

(Benefit mindset lessons can be grounded in academic standards. Instead of a traditional summary, this step can assess students' comprehension of the story.)

2. Acknowledging Feelings

Students ask the character to identify their most persistent distressing thoughts and help them understand how those thoughts influence how they feel. The link between one's thoughts and their feelings is profound, and experience with this fact helps students maintain a more positive attitude in order to better regulate their emotions.

(Here students move from basic comprehension to making inferences as they read between the lines to identify characters' underlying emotions.)

3. Analyzing Actions

Students assist the character in realizing their actions are often a reaction to how they feel. However, their choices actually may be making things worse, and their anger may be directed at the wrong people. This link between feelings and responses is an important lesson for all students who are learning to manage their unpleasant feelings.

(Moving higher on Bloom's Taxonomy, students now deeply examine key plot developments.)

4. Moving Forward

Students encourage the character to socialize with positive people and to help others. Bringing characters outside of themselves as they shift their focus from their own pain and past toward the needs of others reveals the healing components of a benefit mindset. Students support the character in moving from excuses and victimhood to surviving and thriving.

(In this step, students problem solve, create viable solutions, and offer ways to be of benefit to others for the character to consider.)

Getting Personal

The main goal of engaging in this type of creative literary dialogue is so every student can vicariously participate in the process of finding hope and healing. Even though it's called Character Therapy and not self-therapy, there's a great deal of social-emotional learning that occurs whenever students find role models who successfully work through their suffering and sorrow.

Often, literary characters mirror the pain some students have themselves endured, and allowing each student to choose the character that speaks to them on a personal level only enhances their growth in emotional intelligence. It also gives students the satisfaction of knowing they've been a part of someone else's healing process, even if only on an imaginary level, and provides faith and comfort in knowing that if others can move beyond adversity, so can they.

While each student is free to disclose personal details and anecdotes while writing these dialogues, the focus is always on helping the character talk through their problems. Therefore, any student self-revelation should occur organically, be relevant to the character's experiences, and be based on each student's comfort level. If certain students experience any type of catharsis by opening up to a character, this only enhances this process; but such self-disclosure is neither necessary nor required.

In fact, we must heed the warning of Shawn Ginwright, Ph.D. (2018): "The term trauma informed care runs the risk of focusing on the treatment of pathology (trauma), rather than fostering the possibility (well-being)." We must be careful not to allow trauma or "the worst thing that ever happened to you" define anyone, especially a child. Educators and parents can use the benefit mindset to teach kids to move beyond bad experiences to a place of self-healing, a big part of which occurs when we also focus on the healing of others.

***

Parents and the public want teachers to focus on the whole child more than ever. Character Therapy is a great way English language arts teachers can infuse social-emotional learning and a benefit mindset into their current curriculum and break away from the standard book report or culminating essay.

Active Listening Strategies

Teachers can also provide instruction about active listening and offer students sentence starters to keep their Character Therapy dialogues flowing. The following tips prove to the speaker in both casual and academic conversations that you're not only hearing what they say, you also understand and empathize with their comments and experiences.

Initiating conversations: *I want to listen. Please share with me…*

Continuing dialogue: *I want to understand. Please explain… Tell me more about…*

Offering assistance: *I'm willing to help. Can we discuss…? I'd be happy to support you in… Can we strategize…?*

Reflecting back: *What I'm hearing is… It sounds like you're saying…*

Extending the benefit mindset should never be an encroachment or an overreach. We must be careful not to make assumptions, become an imposition, or offend—no matter how unintentionally—those who we are trying to help. Sensitivity, delicacy, and diplomacy open doors and open hearts of those who are often scared, scarred, or skeptical of another's support.

Examples of Young Adult Books Suitable for Character Therapy

When looking for possible sources of conflict and trauma for characters in young adult literature, the following multicultural books, both classic and contemporary, are a good start. The Character Therapy process also often applies to more than one character within each novel.

- **Abuse, bullying:** *The Outsiders, The Watsons Go to Birmingham—1963, Shiloh, Speak, Wonder, Blubber*

- **Neglect, abandonment, betrayal:** *Don't You Dare Read This, Mrs. Dunphrey; Harry Potter; Matilda*

- **Exclusion, isolation, injustice:** *Roll of Thunder, Hear My Cry; Island of the Blue Dolphins; The Watsons Go to Birmingham—1963; Kira-Kira; If I Stay; Number the Stars; The Diary of Anne Frank*

- **Mental illness, drugs, alcohol:** *That Was Then, This is Now; House of the Scorpion; The Rest of Us Just Live Here; Mosquitoland; Hey, Kiddo*

- **Violence, gangs:** *The Outsiders, House of the Scorpion, Drive-By, Buried Onions*

- **War, disaster, injury, illness:** *Number the Stars, The Diary of Anne Frank, The Book Thief, The Fault in Our Stars, The Clay Marble*

- **Loss—separation, divorce, death, incarceration, homelessness:** *The Outsiders, Hatchet, Maniac Magee, Holes, Harry Potter, Kira-Kira, House of the Scorpion, A Wrinkle in Time, Locomotion, If I Stay, Buried Onions*

Adverse Childhood Experiences (ACE) Test

To begin Character Therapy, each student personally chooses one literary character who has experienced significant adverse childhood experiences. These characters will not be hard to find because young adult books often feature orphans and outsiders, but it's best to start this activity after students have finished reading the entire novel.

To determine the extent of their character's trauma, students can have their character take the ACE test (*National Public Radio*, 2015). This simple ten-question quiz will produce a score on a ten-point scale, with the highest scores indicating the greatest amount and sources of trauma. However, even a character's low score on the ACE test can be indicative of considerable stress and strife.

Because of the sensitive nature of these questions, it's advised that teachers get signed permission slips after parents are provided access to preview the ACE test questions. Nothing on this questionnaire doesn't occur in young adult books, and parents can be assured that any delicate issues have already been appropriately discussed while reading the class novel in question. In addition, students will be cautioned not to dwell upon graphic details but instead to focus on helping the character through their pain, shame, and fear.

Although it's not advised for teachers to tell their students to take the ACE test for themselves, be prepared for some students to do so on their own anyway. Students may even be overheard sharing their personal ACE scores with their classmates, and some students may reveal to their teacher their own traumatic experiences, both past and present.

Therefore, it's wise to inform students in advance that every teacher is a mandated reporter and that this type of reporting is one important way kids in dangerous situations receive the professional help they need. If interacting with the ACE test spurs some students to disclose areas in their lives where they are suffering and to seek support, then this writing assignment has proven as practical and prescient as our current situation of student self-harm, suicides, and shootings demand.

Sample Character Therapy Dialogue with Ponyboy Curtis from *The Outsiders*

Part 1. Speaking Truth

Robert: Hi, Ponyboy. After seeing that your ACE score is 2, I know you're dealing with some hurtful feelings. I really want to listen to you. Please share with me the major sources of pain, shame, or fear that are continuing to haunt, hurt, or hold you back.

Ponyboy: Thank you, Robert. I guess the biggest pain in my life is that my parents died in a car crash eight months ago. My big brother Darry didn't go to college so he could work full time and be the guardian for me and my other brother, Sodapop. Otherwise, we would've all been split up.

Robert: I'm so sorry about losing your parents, Pony. My parents are divorced, but I have no idea what it's like to be an orphan. That was also really nice of Darry to put his dreams on hold for you and Soda. I know Soda also works full time so you can finish high school.

Ponyboy: Yeah, Soda's great, but Darry really doesn't want me around. He loves Soda but hates me. He's always on me for every little thing. He's way more mean than my dad was.

Robert: Oh, life at home must be rough on you. Do you have friends you can count on?

Ponyboy: Yeah, my gang is like a second family. Johnny is my best friend. But Dallas scares me, and Steve thinks I'm a tagalong. Two-Bit is fun, though. The thing is, we always get harassed and beaten up by the Socs. They hate us because we're greasers, but they don't even know us. They jumped me the other day and cut up Johnny real bad a few months ago.

I ended up running away from home because Darry hit me, and that same night Johnny accidentally killed a Soc. It's a long story, but Johnny ended up in the hospital and was paralyzed because of a broken back. Johnny died right in front of me, and I witnessed Dallas commit suicide that same night because he couldn't handle the pain. I don't think I can take much more. My life is a mess, huh?

Part 2. Acknowledging Feelings

Robert: Thanks for your honesty, Ponyboy. It's completely understandable that you have strong, upsetting feelings when four people you were close to passed away very suddenly. I want to understand more. Please explain to me how your thoughts about what has happened to you bring up frequent feelings of anger, anguish, or apathy. What makes you mad, sad, or not care?

Ponyboy: Are you kidding? I'm constantly sad. I don't really get angry as much as I just close off. For a time, I even pretended Johnny and Dallas weren't dead. I just couldn't bear to face the pain.

Part 3. Analyzing Actions

Robert: I want to help you figure this out. Let's discuss how your frequent sad feelings lead you to pursue isolation. What are you running from, and who do you take out your pain on? How does this closing off from others hurt or help you?

Ponyboy: At first, I thought I was running from Darry and he would be glad I was gone. Now I realize he was only being strict and critical because he wanted the best for me. He wanted me to have all the things he had sacrificed for me. He doesn't hate me; he's just so scared of losing someone else he loves that he's been suffocating me instead of encouraging me. I still don't like how he gets sometimes, but I'm learning to squeeze him right back when he nags me—but all in a more loving and joking way. Things are a lot, a lot better between us now.

Robert: I'm so glad things are better at home. What about with dealing with the deaths of Johnny and Dallas?

Ponyboy: That's getting better, too, but that and the deaths of my parents are going to be with me forever. What I now know is I have to live the best life I can in tribute to my friends and to my mom and dad. The last thing they all would want is for me to waste my life in sorrow. That's what Johnny wanted for me and Dallas before he died–

for both of us to live happy, productive lives. And now that I'm the only one left, I have to make something of my life for Johnny and Dallas both—and for my parents. God, I miss them all so much!

Part 4. Moving Forward

Robert: I want to support you in continuing to make better choices. I'm really proud of you, Pony. You're beginning to deal with all this pain so much better. Let's strategize how you can find an even stronger sense of belonging, as well as how you can become a source of benefit to yourself and to others.

Ponyboy: I'm working this out, too. I realized that Steve and Two-Bit come from messed up homes. I can help them stay out of trouble and find good jobs. But my first priority is being there for Soda. I completely overlooked how much pain he was in when his girlfriend, Sandy, got pregnant by another guy and moved to Florida.

Robert: I love how you're focusing on the needs of others as well as yourself. I always find that when I help someone else, I forget about my own troubles for a while and also feel good that I brought some joy or relief to others.

I know that you get put into the high-level classes at school; perhaps you can also consider tutoring kids to earn extra money and to benefit others. I also think being part of the track team is a wonderful way to do something you enjoy, to bond with friends, and to feel part of something greater than yourself.

I truly think you're going to be okay, Ponyboy. Follow Johnny's advice and stay gold.

Ponyboy: Thanks, Robert. I actually feel good talking with you. I know now that "stay gold" means to appreciate what you have. I may not have a lot, and I may have experienced a lot of bad things at a young age, but I do feel lucky for my family and friends and feel positive about my future.

Robert: The pleasure was mine, Mr. Curtis! Feel free to talk to me anytime.

***

As you can see, a student would have to have an intimate knowledge of a book to be able to write an original dialogue such as this. Besides any therapeutic benefits, the insightful, creative writing that the Character Therapy assignment produces proves to a teacher that a student deeply understood and was deeply involved with the book they had read.

Writing from Outside Oneself

Writing from outside of oneself is a very liberating experience. It temporarily distracts and frees us from the personal burdens we carry and from which it sometimes seems we cannot escape. Anxious, unhappy children do not learn optimally, if at all. But instead of resorting to self-harm or harming others, such kids can reap the rewards of living the benefit mindset as they unburden themselves and others.

When we're engaged in any endeavor where the focus is on supporting others (especially in a way that means something to us personally and that we're actually very adept at), we experience a sense of release from all the other worries and trauma that may be negatively affecting our lives. In very real ways, the benefit mindset is the pathway to personal wellbeing, as well as to advancing the public welfare.

One more writing exercise that helps prepare students for a benefit mindset is to write a story from the perspective of a type of person who they find reprehensible or whose actions they do not agree with or understand. This is a way for students to address stereotypes they may hold and to begin to have empathy for someone whose beliefs and decisions they have heretofore found impossible to comprehend.

Because this short story will be written from the point of view of someone, real or fictional, the student finds detestable or incomprehensible, this repugnant person actually becomes the protagonist of their story. Push students to consider: *What if the antagonist of a great book became the hero of their own life story?*

By writing the story in the first person point of view with this objectionable person as the narrator, the student is challenged to tell this person's side of the story and to provide compelling explanations for why s/he acts and believes as they do. This creation of a logical, revelatory backstory is a wonderful way for students to honor others' journeys. Rather than a list of excuses, this backstory offers a window into someone's soul, even if it's only a fictional window.

Because this is an exercise in empathy and understanding, students should be cautioned not to choose someone who has committed an atrocity for which there is no ultimate justification. Instead, students can be encouraged to choose someone who many others may admire but who in their eyes acts in and advocates for things that are harmful, exclusionary, prejudiced, or unjust.

This writing assignment should be handled delicately. Students can create a pseudonym for the person they choose so this exercise in understanding doesn't create debate or contention among the class. This is a personal assignment where students explore new perspectives and underlying reasons why some people act in the ways they do.

As with Character Therapy, no one is hurt when students attempt to "walk a mile in another's shoes." Imagining what a person has gone through that led them to a path that someone else finds offensive or downright wrong is part of the bridge-building and healing process. It's also the means by which people of opposite points of view and mindsets begin to find common ground and can work together on problems that are affecting them both.

***

When we say we want students to write with passion and purpose, teachers must ask themselves if they're actually giving students the encouragement and writing prompts that engender such enthusiasm and meaning. The five writing projects offered in this chapter are direct avenues to activating the writing fire and commitment ELA teachers seek. Combine these activities with the great whole-class and independent novels your students are reading, and you'll create an English class that is cohesive and compelling, both in itself and as it relates to the whole child.

Imagine actually being excited to read your students' writing. Imagine peer editors who are excited to read their classmates' work and students who eagerly help each other improve their writing because the meat and meaning contained within their words inspires deep conversations and real food for thought.

The days of imagining are over. This book provides you the roadmap to a rewarding teaching reality.

Chapter 11.

Writing with Sophistication

Have you ever dreaded grading a pile of upward of 150 essays you assumed would be filled with the uninspired ramblings of students who couldn't care less about the craft of writing, let alone the topic of their composition?

Writing Complex Sentences Develops Substance and Style in Student Essays

As I wrote in this article for *Edutopia* (2018d), when every student writes on the same topic, you often see a limited number of examples and evidence supporting their similar theses. But this certainly doesn't necessitate each essay being identical to the next in form and substance. You can give your students tools that allow them to dazzle you with their eloquence, even when their viewpoints are similar. Showing students how to use complex sentences and make inferences can transform students' attitudes about and achievement with writing.

The Power of Complex Sentences

An article from *The Atlantic Monthly* (Tyre, 2012) titled "The Writing Revolution" has had the biggest impact on my writing instruction. That article inspired me to move my students from writing simple and compound sentences toward writing complex sentences.

When students join two related ideas in one sentence, writing refinement and depth begin to occur. This isn't to say there won't be a long learning curve as students practice writing more sophisticated sentences. But with lots of modelling and feedback, every student will meet the Common Core standard of "producing simple, compound, and complex sentences" beginning in grade 3 and "varying sentence patterns for meaning, reader/listener interest, and style" beginning in grade 6.

Creating complex sentences is different from taking two simple sentences and combining them with a conjunction to form a compound sentence. Without a formal discussion about independent and dependent clauses, I simply tell my eighth graders to look at the complex sentence starters and examples I provide them, and to try out the ones that seem the most logical way to convey the important idea they want to express. Rather than speaking in the abstract, I find it easier to provide effective feedback and direction when I have a student's concrete attempt to refer to.

Moving from Mere Explanation to Inference

Many students have been taught to justify their examples and evidence using sentence starters like: "This shows that…" or "This evidence relates back to my thesis because…." This simple method of explaining does provide a foundation for developing writers, but I find it to be redundant because it doesn't move their ideas forward or provide depth. Essays are not mere reports; they should be insightful passion pieces the author is invested in and informed about.

Yet adding depth and distinction to student essays isn't an insurmountable challenge. We can move students past the mere regurgitation of knowledge and toward making inferences by encouraging them to use complex sentences.

As with our class discussions, I show my students how to read between the lines of their evidence and make an inference that takes the reader deeper into their topic. I want students to say something important or insightful that most people wouldn't immediately notice about that topic. These inferences often show cause and effect, as well as explain why or how something occurred (Paul and Elder, 2012).

Complex Sentence Starters for Inference

Here are the stems for complex sentences I give my students, along with my own examples of how they might be used.

Since _____, _____.

Since complex sentences join two related ideas, these thoughts must be separated by a comma that is place between each idea.

In order to _____, _____.

In order to include a personal point of view in an essay, add an inference that takes the discussion of the topic below the surface and exposes important insights and opinions.

So that _____, _____.

So that students receive sufficient practice with writing complex sentences, they can be encouraged to include at least one inference in each body paragraph.

On account of _____, _____.

On account of the difficulty some students may initially have with writing complex sentences, it helps when the teacher or a peer editor approves each paragraph before students move on to the next paragraph. This way, mistakes are caught early and successes are capitalized upon.

Because _____, _____.

Because students have the freedom to read between the lines of their evidence, their inferences may reflect an increased ownership of and engagement with their writing.

By _____, _____.

By trusting that even a developing writer has something unique and perceptive to say if given the chance and proper guidance, all student writers can be encouraged and assisted in expressing their voice with confidence and clarity.

After _____, _____.

After students master writing complex sentences, they are better prepared to avoid rambling and run-on sentences and to instead write with greater precision and brevity.

***

After reading *Roll of Thunder, Hear My Cry*, I have my students write an essay about it. Here's an example of how practice with writing complex sentences helped one of my students improve their essay.

Simple sentence: *The Logan family went through a lot.*

Compound sentence: *The Logan family went through a lot, but they ended up safe and strong.*

Complex sentence with inference: *Because Mama and Papa Logan showed dignity and perseverance through the hardships and racism of the Great Depression, their children were better prepared for the challenges of the Civil Rights Movement to come.*

You can see that through my students' continual practice with inference and literary themes, as well as through the films we view together, they are able to compose eloquent sentences full of insight and depth about the books we read.

Forming a personal writing style is an ongoing quest that develops with experience, maturity, and clarity of purpose and perspective. Teachers of every content area can begin contributing to this process, so share these techniques with your interdisciplinary teams. My students' writing and thinking have vastly improved using this strategy, and now I truly enjoy reading their thoughtful, profound essays.

Writing Responses and Conclusions

Since all essays require some type of analysis, opinion, or argument on the part of the writer, teachers of every subject must provide strategies that allow students to express themselves with both scholarship and passion. Instead of waiting until the final paragraph of their essay, however, students can also add their appropriate responses and conclusions within each body paragraph. When these personal reflections and evaluations are written in the form of complex sentences, students infuse their writing with a perceptiveness, investment, and refinement that make their writing shine.

I encourage my students to wrap up their paragraphs and essays by providing their own reaction or viewpoint to the topic, especially as it relates to the specific evidence they're discussing. I want them to move the conversation forward in a meaningful, insightful way—without going backwards or merely repeating what they've already written.

Here are four ways your students can add their personal responses or conclusions to their essays by using complex sentences:

1. Comment

This first avenue of response allows the student to comment on the text. Give your students the image of a thought cloud to signify that they may now express their own ideas concerning the text. They are to reflect on the text and may extrapolate by recommending solutions or offering advice as they discuss the parts that struck them as personally significant. They may also make predictions or speculate on the possible implications of the author's message.

Explain your thoughts, opinions, predictions, or feelings about your essay, examples, or evidence. Here are ways to add your comment, advice, suggestion, or belief:

Unless _____, _____.

Until _____, _____.

Instead of _____, _____.

With regard to _____, _____.

Here are ways to add your ideas about possibility, probability, or condition:

If _____, _____.

When _____, _____.

In the event that _____, _____.

In case _____, _____.

Without _____, _____.

Examples of complex sentences that show commentary:

Until a person can write about their beliefs and opinions with confidence and clarity, they will not be ready for the demands of college.

If you take the time to think deeply about your personal thoughts regarding your essay topic, you will write intelligent responses that take the reader beyond a surface exploration of your thesis.

Instead of expressing your personal views in the first person using "I" statements, you can still say exactly what you think while writing in a more formal and scholarly style that uses the third person.

2. Connect or Compare

Another avenue of response involves something the fascinating teacher asks their students to do all the time, to connect and compare. Give your students the image of an eye to indicate that they're to explain "Where I have seen this before."

Making associations and offering appropriate analogies is what you should be frequently asking your students to seek out. Describing insightful relationships between seemingly disparate texts or examples is thinking of the highest order. Patterns and parallels reveal connections that tie together both knowledge and experience into a brilliant bond that's lasting and eminently worthy of sharing.

As you take your students far away from the familiar as many times as possible with each new novel, link them back to previous books to see the relationships among them. The opportunity to respond allows your students to make those comparisons *for themselves*. Moreover, the continual chance to respond is also always open to your students by making a connection to their own lives and experiences.

Such connections are nothing less than a valid, vital, and utterly scholarly endeavor. For what your students begin to understand is that the personal is actually universal;

only the particulars are different. Those pesky particulars in fact are merely illusions that tend to blind us to the reality that we're all one: Throughout history and despite geography, we're all linked by common experiences, struggles, successes, and dreams. Your students' experiences and opinions are absolutely on par with those recounted in any text or textbook and are equally worthy of exploring and documenting.

Getting students to cite examples and evidence that are accurate and adequate is one thing, but making sure this information is above all *appropriate or relevant* can be a huge challenge. Therefore, giving your students frequent opportunities to create their own responses and to also explain the relevance to the topic at hand is a good way to reinforce this sometimes-difficult skill.

You want your students to constantly be making their own appropriate connections so this skill becomes second nature to them. Then, when their teachers ask students to provide relevant evidence to something complex and perhaps not of the greatest import or interest to them (especially in a standardized testing situation), students still will be adept at citing appropriate links and relationships to the topic.

Compare your evidence to something relevant that you know, and explain the importance of this connection. Here are ways to point out similarities:

Just as/like _____, _____.

Exactly like _____, _____.

Similar to _____, _____.

In comparison to _____, _____.

Compared with _____, _____.

Examples of complex sentences that show comparisons:

Just as the difficulty and depth of the texts students read increases each year, so should the quality and complexity of the writing that students produce also increase.

In comparison to weight lifting or long distance running, students should push themselves little by little to make their responses more convincing, thorough, and heartfelt.

3. Counter or Contrast

Asking students to point out how something differs from something else that's relevant is another way to provide fascinating meaning through contrast. As always, the student must also provide an explanation as to the importance or validity of this difference.

Furthermore, in argumentative writing the student will be required to provide a counterclaim to their original claim. Give your students the image of a penny with its heads or tails duality to emphasize that there are two sides to every coin. Here students may offer an opposing or alternate argument to what the author claimed. If they happen to personally agree with the author's claim, they may still present a counterclaim in order to acknowledge a differing point of view. In either case, students swiftly offer a logical rebuttal to any counterclaims they offer.

Explain the way in which your evidence differs from something else that is relevant, and explain the importance of this contrast. For argumentative writing, acknowledge and provide an opposite argument or counterclaim to the original claim in your thesis, and then offer a rebuttal or response that continues to support your original claim. Here are ways to show opposite views or difference:

Although _____, _____.

Even though _____, _____.

Despite _____, _____.

Unlike _____, _____.

In spite of the fact that _____, _____.

Regardless of _____, _____.

Even if _____, _____.

While _____, _____.

No matter how/that _____, _____.

Examples of complex sentences that show contrast or a counterargument:

Although some students may think of writing as a chore to be completed hastily, they can learn to love writing by looking on it as an opportunity to show off what they understand, as well as to express what they truly believe.

Regardless of how shy or unimportant one may think they are, everyone has personal opinions, ideas, and experiences that should be shared with the world in a thoughtful and intelligent way.

Even if some students do not know or understand everything, they still can display intelligence and expertise by featuring what they are sure of and what they personally think about their topic.

4. Critique

Another avenue of response is allowing your students to critique the text. Give your students the image of a scale or a balance to show them that they are now weighing the validity and importance of the author's ideas. They are to rate, evaluate, and judge the text using their own opinions, background knowledge, or research.

Students are at liberty to distinguish fact from opinion in the piece and are to assess the credibility of the author's claims. Using as many synonyms as you can, encourage your students to evaluate the author's ideas, examples, and evidence based upon three key factors:

Is what the author saying *sound, accurate, and true*? If so, is it also *relevant, appropriate, and does it match* with what they are claiming? Finally, is the author giving the reader *sufficient, adequate, and enough* information to make their case?

You don't want to give your students the impression that they're there only to poke holes in an author's argument or to disparage the author's efforts. Critiquing is not about tearing down. It's about being constructive and civil. Oftentimes, a critique is a love letter to the author for their brilliance, wisdom, and artistry. Encourage your students to think of critiquing as a positive endeavor, even when finding a degree of fault or expressing disagreement.

Evaluate and explain your judgments about your topic, especially as to whether another's reasons and evidence were appropriate, accurate, and adequate. Critique differs from criticism in that it points out both the positive and negative aspects of what you are evaluating. Here are ways to convey judgement in your writing:

Taking into account _____, _____.

By virtue of _____, _____.

Due to the lack of _____, _____.

Due to the abundance of _____, _____.

Without the _____, _____.

Knowing that _____, _____.

In light of the fact that _____, _____.

Putting aside _____, _____.

Examples of complex sentences that show critique:

Due to the lack of complex sentences and responses in the student's essay, the teacher had no choice but to assess it as only partially proficient.

In light of the fact that these suggestions give students a clear path to write a well-organized and intelligent essay, the teacher holds all students to a very high standard for the quality and depth of work they complete.

Knowing that some teachers think an essay should only contain facts, examples, and evidence, students should still confidently defend their right to include their relevant opinions, thoughts, and insights about their topics.

If you want student essays to mean something, be sure you give your students the strategies and encouragement to infuse their writing with personal meaning!

The Dreaded Concluding Paragraph

How many times have we as teachers wanted to push our student writers below the surface or beyond the obvious but had no concrete strategies for them to do so?

The following writing approach provides every student, regardless of any current writing weaknesses, with a wealth of new ideas and profound perspectives for which to transform ordinary writing into extraordinary authorship!

One of the most difficult writing skills for many students to grasp is finding ways to bring their essays to a satisfactory close. Even after mastering the foundations of organization, cohesion, and clarity, my middle school students often need concrete strategies for creating compelling conclusions and apt titles for their various essays.

I created the following Conclusions and Titles brainstorming activity so all of my students could efficiently write a set of six conclusions and coordinating titles for their individual essays and from which they could choose the very best title and conclusion to bookmark their compositions.

I always require every student to complete all twelve items in this exercise, even in the cases when they've already zeroed in on which strategy they think will be most effective. I've found that when students commit to exploring multiple possibilities and are required to write down several ideas, this opens up new insights and approaches that many young writers may have overlooked or may have too hastily dismissed.

Armed with this collection of ideas, my students can then make an informed decision as to which conclusion and title option they like best, or I can help them winnow it down to the top two so the final decision isn't too overwhelming for them.

Often, students end up incorporating some of their unused conclusion ideas within the body of their essays, so this structured brainstorming activity is always time well spent and fruitful in several ways. Besides producing some truly intriguing titles and though-provoking conclusions, this exercise generates fresh perspectives and additional insights students can and should use throughout their essays, even when they think they are "done" or presume to have exhausted all possibilities.

After their final title and conclusion choice has been made, students can develop their initial idea into a fleshed out concluding paragraph that also contains a connection to an effective title. Of course, the full meaning and impact of the link between the title and the conclusion may not become apparent to the reader until the very end of the essay, and this extra level of depth only adds to the creative experience of writing. Suddenly, the craft, artistry, and importance of true essay writing become even clearer to my students, and their personal investment increases accordingly.

Differentiating Writing Instruction

Differentiated instruction is especially crucial in my classroom because I have many students who have IEPs and/or who are English Language Learners. Some of these students need reinforcement or intervention in the fundamentals of writing. Some kids never were taught the essentials, some need it taught again, and some need it to be taught differently (or better). Many just need a consistently supportive setting where they eventually dare to trust their teacher, as well as themselves.

Therefore, you will see that steps 1 and 2 of the following Conclusions and Titles brainstorming activity elicit only the most basic type of conclusion and title. I always quickly guide my students beyond simple recall and regurgitation, but it doesn't hurt any student, even the most advanced, to begin this exercise refocusing and reflecting on the main ideas and points of their essays. Students cannot successfully move beyond or move below the surface if they haven't already clearly comprehended and cohesively conveyed their topic, thesis, and main ideas or points.

This type of differentiated instruction has served my varied students well. I have made significant progress with students with extremely low skills, as well as with students who were clearly advanced. Some may call some of my writing scaffolds "formulaic," but I would call them necessary, albeit temporary, *foundations* that allow all students to immediately express their ideas with coherence and to find their voice with confidence—all while they are also developing in the basic nuts and bolts of writing.

Creating Compelling Conclusions and Titles

I use the following definitions for conclusions and titles so my students have a clear understanding of the purpose and potential of a strong opening and closing to their writing.

- **Conclusions** wrap up, summarize, or provide a satisfactory ending for your essay. They also can provide a deeper meaning or purpose for the reader of your essay.

- **Titles** are "snappy, catchy, short, gripping, and fit" (Nancie Atwell). They should hook your reader into your essay by being dramatic, interesting, mysterious, challenging, or clever.

- Consider using **alliteration** (the purposeful repetition of the same sound or letter at the beginning of words) in your title.

- Titles often have a **deeper meaning** that may not be revealed until the conclusion, so it is best to write your title choices *after* each conclusion option.

- Center the title in the middle of the first line. Capitalize the first letter of every important word. Do not underline the title of an essay. Use quotation marks only if your title contains dialogue (words someone is speaking).

Here is the writing exercise and brainstorming activity I give to my students:

Twelve Ways to Create Engaging Titles and Effective Conclusions

Remind me! Tell me again!

1.) Write a conclusion that restates the major points of your entire essay (your thesis statement, topic, main ideas, or major examples) using different words.

2.) Create a title that tells about your thesis or examples in a few words.

Conclusion transitions to show an ending or to summarize your essay: *In conclusion, To conclude, In summary, To summarize, To sum up, In short, In brief, On the whole, As I have stated, As you can see, Therefore, Finally, In the end,*

Advise me! Help me! Challenge me!

3.) Write a conclusion that suggests, tells, or compels your reader to *do* something after they have read your essay. Writing this conclusion in the form of a question may be very effective to get your reader to take action.

4.) Create a title that works well with what your conclusion is telling the reader to do.

Teach me! Change my mind! Enlighten me!

5.) Write a conclusion that suggests, tells, or compels your reader to *think* or think about something after they have read your essay. Open your reader's mind, change their beliefs, and/or make them believe something new. You must effectively convey why your topic should be as important to your reader as it is to you. Writing this conclusion in the form of a question may be very effective to get your reader to think.

6.) Create a title that works well with what your conclusion is telling the reader to think.

Change my attitude! Make me care! Move me!

7.) Write a conclusion that suggests, tells, or compels your reader to *feel* a certain emotion after they have read your essay. Writing this conclusion in the form of a question may be very effective to get your reader to feel and respond.

8.) Create a title that works well with what your conclusion is telling the reader to feel.

Continue to interest me! Excite me! Inspire me!

9.) Write a conclusion that tells your reader *something interesting* that you have not already said in your essay. You may want to shock or amaze your reader with a new fact or opinion. You may want to make your reader wonder about or want to know more about your topic. Writing this conclusion using a quotation or by making a prediction about your topic may be very effective.

10.) Create a title that works well with the new and interesting/amazing fact, opinion, or prediction that your conclusion offered your reader.

Make me laugh or smile! Cheer me up! Give me hope!

11.) Write a conclusion that is *funny, makes a small joke, or leaves your reader in a good or hopeful mood* after reading your essay. Even though your topic may be very serious or grim, you may still want to leave your reader with hope or a way to look on the bright side.

12.) Create a title that works well with your humorous or hopeful conclusion.

The Lead

Besides a great title, I teach my students to begin their essays with a lead.

A lead is like a ten-second commercial to get your reader interested in your essay. Try asking your reader one of these direct questions or statements:

Did you know…?   *Are you aware…?*

Can you believe…?   *Have you ever…?*

Wouldn't you…?   *Imagine if…*

Using Mentor Texts with this Activity

Teachers can initially model the Conclusions and Titles activity by showing their students mentor texts that contain a clear conclusion. However, remove the author's title and entire conclusion from the mentor text before you present it to the students. Now you can have the entire class come to consensus and complete the Conclusions and Titles brainstorming activity for this mentor text. This modeling can be done together as a whole class and as one very large collaborative group.

You can also reinforce this skill by having small groups, partners, or individuals create amazing titles and conclusions for other mentor texts and then share their best, fully developed ideas with the class. If you like, the class can vote on the ones they like best.

Of course, with all these possible groupings, the big payoff comes when you finally reveal the author's original title and conclusion. With practice, don't be surprised when your students write titles and conclusions that stand toe to toe with those of the author—and in some cases, that surpass what the author wrote!

There's built-in engagement and investment is these activities as the students strive to outdo their classmates and the author. In addition, students are learning a valuable lesson: Even when the class is assigned the same writing topic or task, there are multiple avenues each writer can take. There are also equally valid and compelling ways to approach a common topic that allow for multiple outlooks and insights, creativity and conclusion.

Another way you could reinforce this skill is to work backwards. Provide students with an unaltered mentor text and have the students try to match the type of conclusion the author wrote with one of the six offered in this exercise. If they decide that the author's conclusion is a whole new category, you can have them add that to their brainstorming possibilities. (I would love to hear of more conclusion ideas, so please share!)

Modeling: Seeing this Activity in Action

In my ongoing effort to walk my talk—done to ensure my credibility as much as it is done out of sheer necessity—I will now model the Conclusions and Titles brainstorming activity for you using this chapter section as an example. Here are the six sets of potential conclusions followed by their companion titles that this exercise inspired for this section on writing conclusions:

Remind me! Tell me again!

As you can see, my Creating Conclusions and Titles brainstorming activity is an effective way of differentiating your writing instruction that meets the varying needs of your students so they all can express their ideas articulately and engagingly.

Title: *Engineering Articulate and Engaging Essay Endings and Appellations*

Advise me! Help me! Challenge me!

In order to take your students' writing to the next level, I encourage you to use this fascinating strategy with your students. They will enjoy analyzing and augmenting mentor texts and will feel more confident in bringing their own essays to a gratifying close. Try it with your students, and let me know how it helped or how you made this activity work even better!

Title: *Bright Beginnings and Happy Endings*

Teach me! Change my mind! Enlighten me!

Providing students with structures and strategies to improve their writing is the intentional, scaffolded instructional approach from which all kids can benefit. We do our students a disservice when we expect them to fly too soon without the proper preparation and tools. Breaking down and chunking that what has been previously challenging for your students is the writing facilitator's job. This Conclusions and Titles exercise is an example of such facilitation, and whichever path you choose, you must provide your students with a strong writing foundation.

Have confidence that students will not hesitate to tell you when they no longer need to depend on certain strategies—and some students will simply forge ahead and spread their wings without a word of warning or request for permission! It's not that any of them do not still need your guidance, support, and feedback, it's that they now need their teacher on a progressively more complex and profound level.

As true facilitators, we must not hesitate to provide our students with a solid foundation in all areas, especially in writing. Only then can they increasingly move forward and impress us, as well as themselves, with their burgeoning independence and achievement!

Title: *The Structure of Style*

Change my attitude! Make me care! Move me!

Other subjects are not called science arts, math arts, or history arts; only English language arts enjoys that honor and responsibility. In what significant ways do you consider yourself an arts instructor? How might you and you students find increased joy, meaning, and purpose with a dedicated emphasis on what is artistic and creative about all forms of writing?

Title: *Language Arts Writing Instruction*

Continue to interest me! Excite me! Inspire me!

How do writers distinguish themselves? Why bother to write at all if you're only rehashing what countless others have said before you?

The answer, of course, is to find and refine your voice so that what you write becomes uniquely you. I struggled with this while writing my first book for teachers. What do I, an ordinary classroom teacher, have to add to the education discussion? I had to overcome my self-doubt in order to confidently convey what inside of me was desperately waiting to be expressed.

This issue of confidence cannot be overstated. All writers, especially students, need to learn to write with an authority and assurance that allows their ideas to flow and that draws their reader in. Through the combination of my encouragement and guidance, my students begin to accept that their words have power and that their insights have merit.

Some students may not know or understand everything yet, but my students certainly have valid opinions and ideas about many important issues that they must share with the world. Only then do they become brave enough to say what they really think and feel. Suddenly, their writing shines and captivates! Suddenly, their writing efficacy feeds their overall self-confidence!

Title: *Giving Students Voice*

Make me laugh or smile! Cheer me up! Give me hope!

It is especially intimidating to write for other educators and writers. I find myself constantly looking over my shoulder and second-guessing my every literary choice. Yet teachers who are also writers are wonderfully empathetic to their student's writing hesitations and struggles. They provide their students with the kinds of feedback, encouragement, and strategies they know work because they have found those things valuable and essential for themselves.

I knew this was a proven, effective strategy for my students; but when I came up with the idea to self-model this activity for this book, I wondered if it would suddenly fall short in a professional setting. As I am writing this, I am happily astonished to find that it is indeed a powerful tool for all writers, young and old!

Can you see that many of my conclusion ideas could be incorporated into this section of the book and only enhance my message and meaning? Which one of my conclusions and titles do you like best?

Title: *Save the Best for Last*

Final Words

I never wanted to be a middle school teacher. I always imagined myself teaching high school seniors in Honors/AP English. So when I began my first job in 1993 teaching 8th graders at a severely low-performing school, I knew it would be a temporary assignment.

Little did I know that I would come to love middle school kids and to love the books written specifically for adolescents. I had no idea these books were so profound and so brutally honest about the human condition. I also didn't know kids this age were capable of such startling insight or deep compassion.

Maybe it was an uphill climb to win my students over, but I was won over by them in short order.

We never read any whole-class novels when I was in middle school. All we did was read the stories from the textbook (none of which captivated me), take weekly vocabulary tests (all of which came from random word lists), and do endless exercises in the grammar book (the bulk of which consisted of diagraming sentences).

As a teacher, there was no way I was going to teach the textbook, so by default I turned to the reading of whole-class novels. From the dark recesses of my school's disaster of a bookroom, I would cobble together ragged class sets of books that looked interesting, none of which I had read before. Without cassette tapes of these books (this was pre-internet, folks—no Amazon two-day shipping and no downloads), I was forced to read these books aloud to my students five periods a day.

Period 1 always received the benefit of seeing my very first reactions to these books:

How I was *wrecked* when I saw Johnny die in the hospital, how I couldn't speak through my tears when Bradley reads the letter from Carla, how I screamed when Zero was actually Hector Zeroni, how I was astounded that Maniac abandoned Russel and Piper, how I had no idea that Papa himself had set the cotton on fire, how I agonized if the moose, mosquitos, and tornado all in one day would spell the end of Brian…

The thing was: I ended up crying and laughing and gasping *every time* we read these books, whether it was first period or fifth, whether it was me reading aloud or while listening to the audio recording for the 100th time. I *love* these books.

When I retire soon, my teaching copies of my class novels are going on a special bookshelf in my home office where I can hold them, thumb through them, and get swept right back into their stirring stories and cherished characters.

And I know that part of the reliving of these great books will include echoes of students past, speaking some of the most gratifying words an English teacher can ever hear from his students:

"Are we reading today?!"

"Can't we read just one more page???"

"At first, I thought this book was boring. But you always make reading so interesting. Now I love this book!"

"The book was *way better* than the movie!"

"I never like reading until your class…"

My hope is that, school year after school year, you'll hear these same words from your students as you reach the whole child by teaching whole-class novels.

References

60 Minutes. (2018, March 11). Treating childhood trauma. Oprah Winfrey, correspondent. Retrieved from https://www.cbsnews.com/news/oprah-winfrey-treating-childhood-trauma/.

Begley, S. (2017, October 9). Paradise lost: The mysterious case of the missing utopian novels. *Time.*

Bruner, R. (2001). Repetition is the first principle of all learning. University of Virginia. Retrieved from https://www.researchgate.net/publication/228318502_Repetition_is_the_First_Principle_of_All_Learning.

Davis, M. (2013). 7 teaching resources on film literacy. *Edutopia.* Retrieved from https://www.edutopia.org/blog/academy-awards-film-literacy-resources-matthew-davis.

Dweck, C. (2006). *Mindset: The new psychology of success.* New York, NY: Ballantine Books.

Dweck, C. (2016). Recognizing and overcoming false growth mindset. *Edutopia.* Retrieved from https://www.edutopia.org/blog/recognizing-overcoming-false-growth-mindset-carol-dweck.

Education Week. (2018). A growth mindset is not enough; it's time for a benefit mindset. Commentary by Bokas, A. and Ward, R. Retrieved from https://www.edweek.org/ew/articles/2018/06/20/a-growth-mindset-isnt-enough-its-time.html.

Edutopia. (2016). Bring excitement into any lesson. Ward, R. Retrieved from https://www.edutopia.org/article/bring-excitement-into-any-lesson-robert-ward.

Edutopia. (2017a). Getting everyone on the same page. Ward, R. Retrieved from https://www.edutopia.org/article/getting-everyone-same-page.

Edutopia. (2017b). Young adult novels that teach a growth mindset. Ward, R. Retrieved from https://www.edutopia.org/article/young-adult-novels-teach-growth-mindset-robert-ward.

Edutopia. (2018a). Exploring the benefit mindset. Ward, R. Retrieved from https://www.edutopia.org/article/exploring-benefit-mindset.

Edutopia. (2018b). Showing students the power of words. Ward, R. Retrieved from https://www.edutopia.org/article/showing-students-power-words.

Edutopia (2018c). Life lessons from fictional characters. Ward, R. Retrieved from https://www.edutopia.org/article/life-lessons-fictional-characters.

Edutopia. (2018d). Scaffolding complex sentences. Ward, R. Retrieved from https://www.edutopia.org/article/scaffolding-complex-sentences.

Ellsworth, J. (2001). Teacher as facilitator. Northern Arizona University. Retrieved from http://jan.ucc.nau.edu/jde7/ese425/eco/optional/facilitator.html.

Gallo, C. (2018). Jeff bezos banned powerpoint in meetings. His replacement is brilliant. *Inc.* Retrieved from https://www.inc.com/carmine-gallo/jeff-bezos-bans-powerpoint-in-meetings-his-replacement-is-brilliant.html.

Ginwright, S. (2018). The future of healing: Shifting from trauma informed care to healing centered engagement. *Medium.* Retrieved from https://medium.com/@ginwright/the-future-of-healing-shifting-from-trauma-informed-care-to-healing-centered-engagement-634f557ce69c.

Gordon, B. (2017). *No more fake reading.* Thousand Oaks, CA: Corwin.

Grafwallner, P. (2017). Struggling reluctantly. NCTE. Retrieved from http://www2.ncte.org/blog/2017/03/struggling-reluctantly/.

Jody and Shara. (2016). Helping students learn to cite their sources. *MiddleWeb.* Retrieved from https://www.middleweb.com/25179/how-we-learned-to-cite-our-sources/.

KQED In the Classroom. (2018). Teaching film as literature. R. Ward. Retrieved from https://ww2.kqed.org/education/2018/06/12/teaching-film-as-literature/.

KQED Mind/Shift. (2018). The benefits of helping teens identify their purpose in life. Claudia Wallis, *The Hechinger Report.* Retrieved from https://www.kqed.org/mindshift/49937/the-benefits-of-helping-teens-identify-purpose-in-life.

Kwedor, K. (2019). Words in context: effective strategies for teaching new vocabulary. Retrieved from http://www.ldonline.org/article/65114/.

Minero, E. (2017). When students are traumatized, teachers are too. *Edutopia.* Retrieved from https://www.edut.opia.org/article/when-students-are-traumatized-teachers-are-too.

Mizerny, C. (2016). 10 techniques to teach whole-class novels. *MiddleWeb.* Retrieved from https://www.middleweb.com/30409/10-techniques-to-teach-whole-class-novels/.

National Commission on Social, Emotional, and Academic Development. (2017). The evidence base for how we learn: supporting students' social, emotional, and academic development. Retrieved from https://www.aspeninstitute.org/publications/evidence-base-learn/.

National Education Policy Center (2019). Personalized learning and the digital privatization of curriculum and teaching. Retrieved from https://nepc.colorado.edu/publication/personalized-learning.

National Public Radio. (2015). Take the ACE quiz—and learn what it does and doesn't mean. Laura Starecheski. Retrieved from https://www.npr.org/sections/health-shots/2015/03/02/387007941/take-the-ace-quiz-and-learn-what-it-does-and-doesnt-mean.

Nicol, D. and MacFarlane-Dick, D. (2007). Formative assessment and self-regulated learning: a model and seven principles of good feedback practice. pp. 199-218. Retrieved from http://dx.doi.org/10.1080/03075070600572090.

Paul, R. and Elder, L. (2012). Distinguishing between inferences and assumptions. The Foundation for Critical Thinking. Retrieved from https://www.criticalthinking.org/pages/distinguishing-between-inferences-and-assumptions/484.

Potter, K. (2016). Teaching foreshadowing in the secondary English classroom. Retrieved from http://mskcpotter.blogspot.com/2016/08/teaching-foreshadowing-in-secondary.html.

Price-Mitchell, M. (2012). The role of heroes for children. *Roots of Action*. Retrieved from https://www.rootsofaction.com/role-of-heroes-for-children/.

ResourcEd. (2017). Collaborative learning vs. cooperative learning: what's the difference? Retrieved from https://resourced.prometheanworld.com/collaborative-cooperative-learning/.

Rich, J. (2018). The importance of difficult conversations in U.S. classrooms. *The Hechinger Report*. Retrieved from https://hechingerreport.org/the-importance-of-difficult-conversations-in-u-s-classrooms-teaching-about-the-migrant-crisis/.

Ripp, P. (2018). What's in our reader's notebook. Retrieved from https://pernillesripp.com/2018/09/14/whats-in-our-readers-notebook/.

Sacks, A. (2019). Whole-class novels vs. choice reading: why not do both? *Education Week Teacher*. Retrieved from https://www.edweek.org/tm/articles/2019/04/16/whole-class-novels-vs-choice-reading-why-not.html.

Schwartz, K. (2017). How making an impact on the world motivates students. *KQED Mind/Shift*. Retrieved from https://www.kqed.org/mindshift/49341/how-making-an-impact-on-the-world-motivates-students.

Short, K. (2019). Reading aloud to middle school students. Retrieved from https://www.edutopia.org/article/reading-aloud-middle-school-students.

Sweeney, D. (2010). The seven norms of collaborative work. Retrieved from https://dianesweeney.com/the-seven-norms-of-collaborative-work/.

TeachSDGs. (2018). Retrieved from http://www.teachsdgs.org/.

Truby, D. (2019). 11 essential tips for teaching theme in language arts. *We Are Teachers*. Retrieved from https://www.weareteachers.com/11-tips-for-teaching-about-theme-in-language-arts/.

Tyre, P. (2012). The writing revolution. *The Atlantic*. Retrieved from https://www.theatlantic.com/magazine/archive/2012/10/the-writing-revolution/309090/.

U.S. Dept. of Education. (2016). Gratitude, grit, and a growth mindset. R. Ward. *The Teachers Edition*. Retrieved from https://content.govdelivery.com/accounts/USED/bulletins/15c71b4.

Ward, R. (2015). *The firm, fair, fascinating facilitator*. Lanham, MD: Rowman and Littlefield.

Ward, R. (2016). *A teacher's inside advice to parents: How children thrive with leadership, love, laughter, and learning*. Lanham, MD: Rowman and Littlefield.

Ward. R. (2017). *Talented teachers, empowered parents, successful students: classroom strategies for including all families as allies in education*. CreateSpace.

Ward, R. (2018). *Teaching the benefit mindset: moving empathy, inclusion, and altruism to the forefront of education*. Kindle Direct Publishing.

About the Author

Robert Ward is an enthusiastic educator, author, and champion for children, who is currently enjoying his twenty-seventh year teaching English to a wide diversity of students at public middle schools in Los Angeles, CA.

His first book for educators, *The Firm, Fair, Fascinating Facilitator*, and its companion workbook, *The Teacher Tune-Up*, empower teachers to attend to the needs of the whole child. Robert extends his holistic approach to nurturing children in his third book, *A Teacher's Inside Advice to Parents: How Children Thrive with Leadership, Love, Laughter, and Learning*, published by Rowman and Littlefield.

Robert's fourth book, *Talented Teachers, Empowered Parents, Successful Students*, brings his previous writing full circle as he joins teachers and families as allies in education. In *Teaching the Benefit Mindset*, that circle is expanded and fortified by an emphasis on moving empathy, inclusion, and altruism to the forefront of education.

In *Reaching the Whole Child by Teaching Whole-Class Novels*, Robert shares his passion and expertise for how the social, emotional, soulful, academic, and altruistic needs of children can be met through the power of reading great books.

In addition to his award-winning Rewarding Education blog, Robert's articles for educators and parents are regularly featured in Edutopia, Education Week, KQED *In the Classroom*, Smart Brief, ASCD, NCTE, the U.S. Department of Education's "The Teacher's Edition" newsletter, and the International Literacy Association.

Robert has also mentored over 200 teachers at various stages of their careers. His additional leadership roles include a two-year appointment by the State Superintendent of Public Instruction to the Student Learning Subcommittee at the California Department of Education and graduate level teaching experience at California State University, San Bernardino, as an adjunct instructor in the College of Education.

Robert lives in the historic View Park neighborhood of Los Angeles with his husband of twenty-four years and their two incredibly cute doggies. You can contact Robert by email at *misterward@sbcglobal.net*.

Made in the USA
Coppell, TX
08 June 2025

50457544R10083